THE CLASH

ALL THE ALBUMS ★ ALL THE SONGS

Martin Popoff

CONTENTS

INTRODUCTION

"The only band that matters" they said of Joe Strummer, Mick Jones, Paul Simonon, and Topper Headon. But such solemn positioning was won the hard way (that's entertainment!), through jockeying, striving, competition, and envy. The thumping hearts at the pole position beat inside of Mick, Joe, Paul, and manager Bernie Rhodes, who rapidly conspired to create something deserving of that erudite (albeit label-generated) epithet, which, amid the rest of the contemporary punks, could alternately have framed The Clash as "the adults in the room."

Indeed, The Clash rapidly landed at a place of maturity—"Write about issues," Bernie admonished—but in the beginning, it was all about the competitive energy burning inside desperate youth going for broke. And what Mick, first, and then Bernie and then Joe wanted was what the Sex Pistols had: namely, their terrible power on stage and Johnny Rotten's effect on the suddenly formed stylish cult of a mob called punks.

Mick was already a punk on paper at least, having been part of the little-known, controversially named London SS, who through its brief revolving-door tenure, also included Rat Scabies and Brian James (both later of The Damned), along with theoretical bassist Paul Simonon. Mick also had going for him the same sort of quasi-hippie rock aficionado roots as Rotten and Strummer and thus a rich grounding in music that would add depth to the songs he would write.

Joe had a flash of the punk as well, through his fronting of the 101ers, a minor pub rock band about London, and his authority-questioning hippie ideals (he would come to understand that punks and longhairs were one and the same). Once Joe witnessed the Pistols, when the 101ers headlined over them at London's Nashville Room on April 3, 1976, he saw the light, confirming his embarrassment at feeling obsolete at just twenty-four years old.

But competitive fire would put The Clash on the track to mattering. Now Mick and Bernie *and* Joe had an adversary in the Sex Pistols. Mick and Bernie had a second adversary in the 101ers and effectively poached Joe (scouted first by Bernie and The Clash's then second guitarist Keith Levene in May 1976), whose own burning sense of purpose already had him primed to jump ship.

A rhythm section seemed secondary to ideology. Terry "Tory Crimes" Chimes would appear on the band's incendiary first record but was soon replaced by Topper Headon. Paul Simonon, a South Londoner, was The Clash's Sid Vicious insomuch as he couldn't play bass, but he'd bloody well figure it out. He was already halfway there—he looked the part, all menacing punk, an anti-pinup pinup in safety pins.

In addition to their rivalry with the Pistols, the band found themselves in dustups with the Stranglers (also self-conscious of age and in need of

OPPOSITE: Joe in his 101ers days. He would come to understand hippies and punks were cut from the same cloth.

HOFNER

ABOVE: Flyer for an early gig, this one at the Royal College of Art, London, November 5, 1976.

LEFT: A Sheila Rock photo appeared on a cover of the *Sniffin' Glue* fanzine in 1977.

purpose), sped up by the energy of the Ramones and Buzzcocks (famously playing a gig with the latter and the Pistols), and resolute in their ambition to play live before The Damned did—poetically, the first Clash gig found them supporting the Pistols on July 4, 1976, up in Sheffield.

The next night, witnessing the Ramones play Dingwalls in London, the band reconfirmed for themselves that punk was *not* homegrown and that it might be better if they competed in the realm of ideas rather than trying to match the Ramones or the New York Dolls or the Sex Pistols on plowing heaviness. If Bernie, Mick, and Joe had to take on all comers, they would, through stratagem and sheer hard work, but also with their natural inclination toward punk politics.

All these considerations helped build a legend of The Clash as rude strivers, as did their signing to CBS for an advance of £100,000, an event that caused Mark Perry of *Sniffin' Glue* magazine to poison-pen his famed quip, "Punk died the day The Clash signed to CBS." Working with heavy metal man Sandy Pearlman on their second album underscored their sense of ambition and the perceived abandonment of punk that would mark the rest of the band's albums, beginning with *London Calling*.

But it is perhaps all of this deliberation and ambition that ultimately made The Clash great. To put it personally, even as a fourteen-year-old kid buying all those first punk albums, I could hear that inside all of the pointy, shouted tracks on *The Clash* a band to be taken more seriously than the Saints, the Ramones, the Dead Boys, and even on some level the Sex Pistols, who seemed comparatively garish and juvenile, from their band name and record title down to their album art and the thespian sneering over stacked power chords that nearly smothered every song into one dimension.

Later, with *London Calling*, The Clash opened my mind, educating me—throwing an arm around me, even—and wrestling me along a path past punk and into myriad artists and albums with current-event politicking on top. When they became—like Bruce Springsteen and later U2—worthy of thoughtful mainstream press in North America (this had happened straightaway in the UK), my buddies and I already knew they deserved to be part of that conversation (we expressed our proud patronage by adding "Tommy Gun" and "Brand New Cadillac" to our hapless bar band's set list).

As the years wore on The Clash provoked further with the layered urban distortion of *Combat Rock* and the Mick- and Topper-less *Cut the Crap* (a break too far). At that point, purpose had been served, and the band imploded. Strummer, with his enthusiasm for grabbing life by the neck and shaking it, ran off and made a solo record, acted, wrote soundtracks, and finally returned renewed and even more maniacally in love with music with his band the Mescaleros. Meanwhile his ex-writing partner, Mick Jones, the sensitive voice and comparatively blissed-out presence, kept us dancing with the quite successful Big Audio Dynamite, a band that was an obvious evolution from The Clash of *Combat Rock*, visionary in their embrace of dance, rap, dub, electronica, and EDM.

Mick performing with his pre-Clash band, Rich Kids

The Clash would never re-form, of course, although tantalizing vague plans were afoot in the mid-'90s and again at the time of Joe's death in 2002. But because it never happened, The Clash's great mythology was established to remain forever intact. In that sense (and a few others), The Clash are the Led Zeppelin of punk and arguably a grade above, even when judged by the hyperbolic "only band that matters."

But it is less hyperbole to note that the rock critics club has written The Clash into a realm inhabited by the likes of Woody Guthrie, Dylan, the Stones, Springsteen, and U2. And for that reason, I'd have to say that a book of sincere and, scholarly song-by-song analysis is wholly warranted by the action-packed intellectual heft of what the band accomplished in less than a decade of almost constant tumult.

In the end, I hope the cornucopia of trivia and detail that necessarily pours from something like this serves to inspire further study. Joe Strummer was all about experience and worldly wonder, and the music he made with The Clash offers an often giddy and always endearing celebration of humanity, urgently croaked and yet so eloquently espoused. He will be missed, as will the band's tight (but loose!) catalog of revolution rock, reggae, and raga.

SIDE 1

JANIE JONES

REMOTE CONTROL

I'M SO BORED WITH THE U.S.A.

WHITE RIOT

HATE & WAR

WHAT'S MY NAME

DENY

LONDON'S BURNING

SIDE 2

CAREER OPPORTUNITIES

CHEAT

PROTEX BLUE

POLICE & THIEVES

48 HOURS

GARAGELAND

Recorded at CBS Studio 3, London, and National Film and Television School, Beaconsfield, UK

Release Dates
April 8, 1977 (UK: CBS S CBS 82000)
July 26, 1979 (US: Epic JE 36060)

Produced by Micky Foote
Engineered by Simon Humphrey

RIAA Certification: Gold
Top *Billboard* Position: No. 126

THE CLASH

JOE STRUMMER
Guitar, Vocals

MICK JONES
Guitar, Vocals

PAUL SIMONON
Bass

TORY CRIMES
Drums

Armed with a record deal within nine months of forming and with just thirty-odd gigs under their belts, The Clash found themselves signed to establishment label CBS for a much-hyped (and some contended tainting) advance of £100,000 for five records. But the deal was not as pretty as it sounded.

No, The Clash hadn't exactly paid their dues, and they were summarily derided for the CBS deal. Nevertheless, they had their short, shocking, and likable songs down by the latter half of 1976, signed their deal on January 25, 1977, and then went into what would be three long weekends' worth of recording sessions (mix included) at CBS Studio 3 in Whitfield Street in February '77 at a total cost of £4,000 (the band was cognizant that the Stooges' *Raw Power* had been recorded here). Producing at CBS Studio 3 was the band's soundman and a connection dating back to the 101ers, Micky Foote, with CBS staffer Simon Humphrey presiding as engineer and Mick bounding in to essentially coproduce.

Gigging was put aside to make the best possible use of the studio time. When the record was completed, manager Bernie Rhodes urged the band to woodshed further in hopes of tightening up their presentation for the dates that would follow the release of the record—in the UK and Europe in April and May, then back to mainland Europe in the summer and fall.

There was also the matter of finding a new drummer.

Excitement built around the band, because although The Damned had managed to get out the first UK punk album, *Damned, Damned, Damned* in February, the Sex Pistols played just a handful of shows in early 1977, battered by bad publicity and bans. Upon its release on April 8, 1977, *The Clash* hit No. 12 on the UK charts and achieved gold certification. Although it wasn't released in the States due to label concerns over its spare production, import sales to the US accounted for about 100,000 copies.

Without much to compare to, the album nevertheless satisfied several punk requirements, even if the music proved more smartly daring and varied than standard-issue punk albums arriving throughout the balance of the year and into 1978. For one thing, the very name of the band screamed punk, as did the scrappy, ragged vibe of the album cover art, on which CBS staffer Roslaw Szaybo captured the beaten morale of the streets with a grainy shot of the band sans drummer (the record's skinsman Terry Chimes had been replaced by Topper Headon just a week prior to the album's release). The photo depicts Mick, Joe, and Paul shot by Kate Simon on the ramp opposite the band's rehearsal space in Camden. Surely, the surly punk buyer probably thought the band was a trio or couldn't get it together enough to show up in the same place at the same time for a photo shoot. The back cover (so punk that it, in fact, presaged hard-core design) presents a Rocco Macauley photo of stampeding bobbies at the 1976 Notting Hill Carnival riot, in which Joe and Paul had participated.

Also "punk" about this first album (somewhat counterintuitively) is the fact that unlike what was coming out of other punk bands—goofball humor, nihilism, general stupidity—The Clash actually spit out substantial mouthfuls regarding myriad economic and political problems, defining better than any other band the bullet points of the punk manifesto. As well, there are plenty of dark, hooligan melodies, another punk signifier, especially to North Americans learning of the English experience through punk—something about English punk (versus American punk) sounded like pub-hollered football anthems. Finally, there still is Joe's crude, unschooled vocal style, in which he made no attempt to mask his accent and which stylistically was an attempt to distance himself from his middle-class roots. Mick didn't mask his accent either, but he sounded like youth and innocence personified, thus creating an obvious contrast and further underscoring the idea of the band as multidimensional and layers deep.

Yet despite multiple punk signals, musically, *The Clash* sounds like the work of a band already envisioning a post-punk world, an effect achieved by transitions, varied vocal arrangements, outlier tracks such as "Police & Thieves," and, most of all, by the record's thin, wiry, frantic guitar sound, the sonic antithesis to what the Sex Pistols would propose on *Never Mind the Bollocks* in late October 1977, six months late to the party (but what party-crashers they were).

The 1976 riots in which Joe and Paul participated in the Notting Hill section of London figured prominently in the debut, most obviously in track four.

JANIE JONES

STRUMMER/JONES 2:05

The Clash's debut LP opens (somewhat incongruously) with a song about infamous British madame Marion Mitchell, who in the 1960s performed as a singer under the stage name Janie Jones.

The Clash opens oddly, with a song about pining for paid sex after the drudgery of a day at the office, the protagonist yearning to jump into his workingman's Ford Cortina rust bucket and pick up Janie Jones for a bit of fun, getting stoned and maybe seeing some rock 'n' roll (or heading to the disco, according to the demo). Though ill-advised at a time of high employment, by tale's end, our working stiff is about to quit his job and tell his boss to shove it. The British colloquialism "lucky lady" is an ironic expression, indicating she may be anything but. Hence, it could be interpreted to mean the worker is going to take out his

frustrations on the lady of the night or, conversely, that he has empathy for their shared plight.

Originally written by Mick in the first person on the Harrow Road bus while on his way to the band's Chalk Farm rehearsal space, "Janie Jones" was one of The Clash's very first compositions. Joe was leery of the boy/girl subject matter and shifted it to the type of third-person vignette one might associate with the Kinks (it's also a device later deployed by The Jam).

n December 1982, the band and some of an Dury's Blockheads would pay homage to ones with a single called "House of the Ju-Ju Queen" (the song was credited to Janie Jones & The Lash).

The Janie Jones to whom Mick referred was the famous British brothel madame Marion Mitchell, who in the 1960s under the stage name Janie Jones was also a cabaret singer known for the 1965 novelty hit "Witches Brew," which reached No. 46 in the charts. In 1974 she was sentenced to seven years for "controlling prostitutes." Mick has noted that at the time of writing, Jones was still very much fodder for the weekly tabloids. The curious line, *There's no payola in his alphabetical file*, could mean the worker resents having to pay for his sex while his bosses are getting it free as a form of payola. Indeed, additional accusations against Jones had her embroiled in a payola scandal allegedly involving the BBC, a band called New World, *Top of the Pops*, Jimmy Savile, other call girls, and various film and TV producers. The scandal was regularly in the news beginning in 1971, ramping up to Jones's incarceration in 1974 and subsequent release in 1977. In December 1982, the band paid homage by recording a single called "House of the Ju-Ju Queen" with Jones and some of Ian Dury's Blockheads (the song was credited to Janie Jones & The Lash).

Musically, one might ascribe a degree of album-opening impact to "Janie Jones," thanks to opening with its anthemic chorus in which Joe chants in a monotone over Chimes's roiling drum pattern. On second go 'round, the bass joins the drums and stabbing chords, and we're off, further fired up by a unison gang vocal introducing what would become a Clash trademark. The song featured in the band's live set from their first gig to their last and virtually every show in between.

REMOTE CONTROL

STRUMMER/JONES 3:00

The story of "Remote Control" is one of wry irony. Mick's lyric expresses frustration with bureaucracy, namely bureaucracy in big business and bureaucracy in government, for the two essentially conspired to hobble and then scuttle much of the 1976 Anarchy Tour (one would think, quite sensibly, to stop anarchy) featuring the Sex Pistols, The Clash, The Damned, and Johnny Thunders and the Heartbreakers. The final nail in the coffin came with the Sex Pistols' label, EMI, pulling tour support. The song's reference to a meeting at Mayfair concerns a meeting of EMI shareholders on December 7, 1976, that resulted in the Pistols being tossed from the label.

The irony is that a song expressing the band's anger at a lack of control was chosen by CBS as a single (backed with a mono live version of "London's Burning," just to restoke the fires of anarchy) *against* the band's wishes (they wanted to release "Janie Jones" and in fact had told *Melody Maker* that "Janie Jones" would be the next single, following "White Riot"). As a

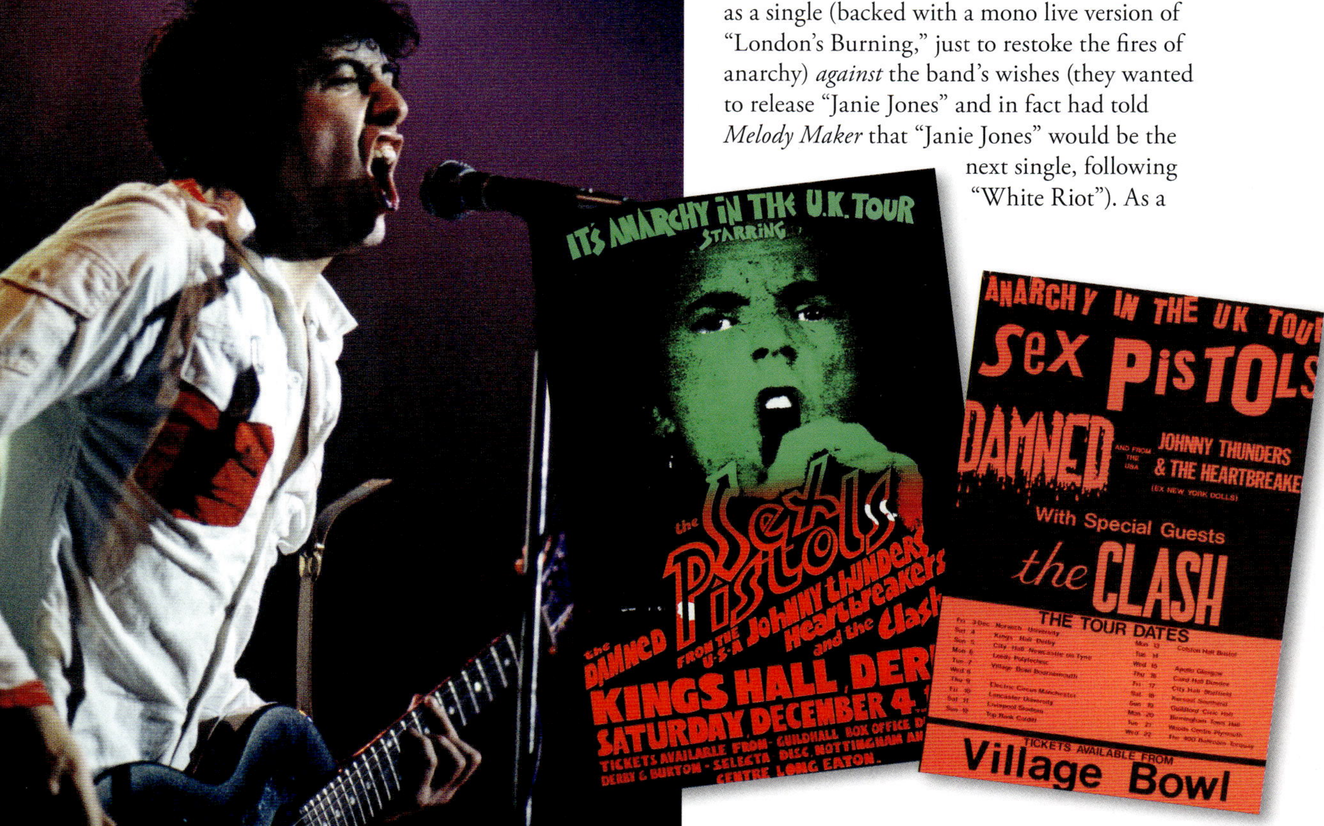

BELOW: Out of Control Tour. With "Remote Control," Mick expressed frustration with the bureaucracies that had scuttled much of the 1976 Anarchy Tour.

"Remote Control" b/w "London's Burning Live)," UK, May 13, 1977.

result, the band quickly built up a distaste for the song—easy pickings, given its almost treacly verse melody—and reminded themselves of the incident with the very first line of response track "Complete Control" (see sidebar, pages 45–46). The band's lack of support for "Remote Control" was communicated to the fans, and as a result, the song failed to chart.

The song includes a sprinkling of amusing references, including panda car (police car), Dalek (Daleks being a repressive race of cyborgs in the *Doctor Who* saga, originally inspired by the Nazis), and an interesting use of the term "punk" in the old-school vernacular, referring to someone who is broke and powerless. The band even managed to squeeze in a complaint about pubs being forced to close at eleven o'clock.

In terms of the musical arrangement, the song's architecture is interesting. Like "Janie Jones," it plots a deftly accessible melody against stabbing, staccato exercises in rhythm (which must've been knees-up fun to execute live)—a rhythm that, in fact, evokes the classic football terrace chant "You're Gonna Get Your Fuckin' Head Kicked In" and here is underscored by handclaps added to the intro and outro.

The band play with time changes too, which, combined with the slick move between pop and pomp, prompted drummer Terry Chimes to remark that Mick had written a "mini opera." As well, we get a vocal from Mick, always the voice of melody, before Joe enters to raise the temperature and sense of menace. Done with the verses, the song transitions into a heroic descending windup of an outro, as the band decries repression, again with terrace vibe but also a sense of resignation, like the home side's down three-nil.

I'M SO BORED WITH THE U.S.A.

STRUMMER/JONES 2:24

Opening with an octave-jumping riff recalling the Pistols' "Pretty Vacant," "I'm So Bored with the U.S.A." quickly lands in familiar Clash terrain, mixing melodic verse riffing with a holler-along hooligan chorus perfect for denting heads at the gig.

Originally titled "I'm So Bored with You," this pre-Clash Mick Jones composition was addressed to the same girlfriend caught lying to him in "Deny." (See page 29.) But according to Joe, while listening to the chorus at the band's squat in Davis Road, he misheard it as an anti-America screed because of people talking while he was trying to soak it in. Those who don't buy Joe's slightly romanticized telling reference another version in which Bernie implored him to change the lyric because he wanted the band to stop writing love songs.

The economy with which Joe transformed the song is remarkable, touching down on Watergate, on Cambodia and the heroin or "skag" usage that devastated the troops there (Black Sabbath covered this topic as well), on American funding of proxy wars and military regimes, and even on the crime wave peaking in the late 1970s, particularly in New York City.

A bit about a murder happening every ten seconds didn't survive past the demo stage (nor did digs at baseball jerseys and all the sleepy music being made in L.A.), but Joe did manage to combine commentary on crime with American junk culture by referencing TV detectives Starsky from *Starsky & Hutch* and the bald-headed Kojak, with the *suck on Kojak* line referring to the character's reliance on lollipops to help him quit smoking. Given that Elvis Costello was listening repeatedly to the first Clash album when crafting his *My Aim Is True* debut, it is up for debate whether "Watching the Detectives" was influenced by "I'm So Bored with the U.S.A." or simply similarly affected by American detective shows on UK airwaves. In any event,

this was the main theme according to Joe, who in later years said the song was essentially about "the importing of culture."

Regarding the song's organically altered title and new subject matter, "punk poet" John Cooper Clarke expressed amusement that anyone could possibly claim to be "bored" with the United States, especially an Englishman in the 1970s. Love it or hate it, sure, but bored by it? Unlikely. Indeed, the vibe here is one of punks being provocative.

Regardless, the sentiment is set to a punk panic of an up-tempo and frantic track, the anger of it all tending to mask the incongruence of Mick's sophisticated lick behind Joe's spit job on the verses. Three tracks in, adding to the reference to "punk" in "Remote Control," "I'm So Bored" finds Joe saluting "the new wave," a likely reference to the burgeoning punk scene taking place at CBGB and Max's Kansas City across the pond in New York, a city he will soon enthusiastically embrace.

Warming up backstage at the Royal College of Art, London, November 5, 1976.

WHITE RIOT

STRUMMER/JONES 1:55

In the spirit of the UK's and punk's singles culture, CBS issued the first Clash single a few weeks in advance of the debut album, namely a version of "White Riot" recorded before the three album sessions and backed with the non-LP track "1977." There's not much difference between these two versions of "White Riot," with the most obvious being the police siren intro on the single, a "1-2-3-4" count-in on the album version, and a slightly modified bassline.

Either way, the song is a scrappy and raucous stomper with the most discipline coming from Paul Simonon, who turns in a tight yet bobbing bassline set against five very distorted chords.

Harlesden Coliseum, London, March 11, 1977.

Lyrically, the song is one of The Clash's many calls to action; in this instance, Joe uses as motivation references to blacks and their street actions, noting that "they don't mind throwing a brick" to call attention to their problems. By contrast, says Strummer, whites are subservient, timid, cowardly, anesthetized by school, and afraid of jail.

The motivation for the song was Strummer's, Simonon's, and manager Bernie Rhodes's involvement in the August 30, 1976, Notting Hill Carnival riot, in which black carnival goers defended themselves against a harassing police presence that numbered up to 1,600 amid already simmering tensions over police practices, such as stop and search. Police and police property took the brunt of the damage in the riot, and the photo on the back of the album commemorates the melee.

Watching the West Indian community rise against the police got Joe to ponder why white people didn't do the same; he infers that the power structure had made life just barely comfortable enough for whites to prevent them from questioning their lot.

Joe's lyric makes an interesting comparison, but calling the song "White Riot" might seem ill-advised. Music fans were generally smart enough not to get the wrong idea, and "White Riot" quickly became a Clash classic. Still, it often caused problems at shows, making the band hesitant to play it and promoters leery of it as well. The band also found themselves having to defend themselves against charges of racism by the notoriously combative press of the day.

Jones most definitely noticed the problem, but he also found the music a little juvenile and obvious as well. In fact, he refused to play it once in 1979 and found himself at the end of a bruising punch from Joe. But the two would come full circle. In 2002, Joe was playing a firefighters' benefit show with Mick in attendance. Joe called Mick on stage for "Bankrobber," "White Riot," and "London's Burning," marking the first time the two played together since the bust-up. A month later, Joe would be dead from a heart attack

"White Riot" b/w "1977," UK, March 18, 1977.

The Clash in Belfast, Northern Ireland, for their Out of Control Tour, October 1977.

HATE & WAR

STRUMMER/JONES 2:04

With "Hate & War," The Clash continued to lay it on heavy, lending punk an irascible fighting spirit, with Joe even citing the song as a response to hippies.

Chipping the walls of society like a machine-gun spray are references to junkies, foreign wars, squatting, cheating to win, aggression, and even equal opportunity hatred against the English, the Greeks, the "wops," and the cops.

The vocal, however, is from Mick, so there's a bit of a disconnect with the violence of it all, underscored by the pub rock verses, the pop chorus, the jangly guitars (one panned left, one panned right, and one right down the middle), and even a fleeting nod to boogie rock. Although Joe is the response to Mick's call, it is mostly Mick's vocal, and his naïve, almost vacant delivery might even be considered more unsettling than if had Joe taken the lead.

But these are Strummer's sentiments. He recalled in interviews that he had put the words together by candlelight in an abandoned ice cream factory that he was using as a squat behind Harrow Road in Foscote Mews, and that he took his work to rehearsals the next day where Mick slammed together the music. Joe took further ownership of the song by painting HATE AND WAR in huge white letters on the back of his jacket, just above HEAVY MANNERS ("under heavy manners" being a reggae term for repression as well as a political slogan). In fact, the lyric mentions "hate and war on my back," which carries the double meaning of literally wearing hate and war and constantly being harassed by it.

A number of ideas here mirror "White Riot," especially the idea that people have got to toughen up and expect a little bloodshed in the fight against the establishment, specifically those letting London, through ineptitude and lack of empathy, rot in the same way as the Big Apple.

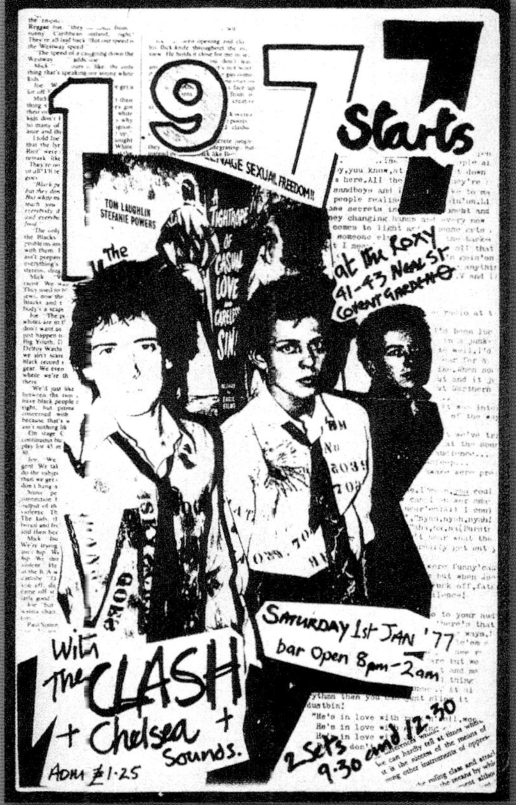

OPPOSITE: "Hate & War" may have featured Mick's vocal, but the sentiments were those of Joe, who recalled writing the song by candlelight in an abandoned ice cream factory.

ABOVE: The Clash opened 1977 with a gig at London's Roxy Club, advertised on this flyer credited to artist Jamie Reid.

WHAT'S MY NAME

STRUMMER/JONES/K.LEVENE 1:40

"Thinking Man's Yobs" on the cover of *New Musical Express*, accompanied by an outtake from the Chalkie Davis photo shoot.

Despite Keith Levene's assertions that he was in on writing many of the songs on the first Clash album, reportedly accomplished in May 1976 at Riverside Studios, "What's My Name" is his only official credit. Joe said that once he joined, he threw in a couple of verses to keep the choruses apart on what is thought to be mostly a collaboration between Keith and Mick.

Over and done in 1:40, the song in fact accomplishes much on the subject of teen alienation, which, after all, is the starter kit for punk alienation. The song's protagonist is dealing with everything from acne (*I tried spot cream*) to existential identity crisis. Problems stem from a busted home life and result first in fighting (and of course getting caught), progressing to breaking and entering. A line perhaps intended to amuse, about trying to join a Ping-Pong club, is in fact the song's most heartbreaking—a yearning for childhood fun and maybe some friends to share it with is thwarted by the club being full-up, and another one is lost to the street.

Musically, this is one of the debut album's most aggressive songs, although it is more so written that way and then botched in the delivery, given the distressingly thin guitar lines and the garage punk chorus. The break is even more ethereal, Joe resigned to mumbling over dropped-out music at 0:54 before a menacing final verse in which our teen protagonist has become a night prowler.

Joe's vocal on "What's My Name" is one of his angriest, while Chimes pounds home a tribal rhythm, going with tom-toms on the verse and eschewing any sort of expected high-hat beat until chorus time. Add it up, and the relentless punk of the song, forced through a compromised arrangement, results in a squalid and gritty urgency that rests below the poverty line of the rest of the album.

DENY

STRUMMER/JONES 3:03

One of the longest songs on the record, "Deny" has got a bit of pub rock to it, even some of the sounds of girl groups of the '60s. That makes sense because it's one of Mick's pre-Clash songs, as well as a boy/girl song, if a bit dark, dealing as it does in shooting smack, along with the usual boy/girl stuff. In this light, it has been speculated that it was a veiled message to early Clash guitarist Keith Levene, who was bounced from the group due to his use of heroin and speed (although Mick was no saint as pertains to the latter). The claim is dubious, considering Keith had not been using needles yet.

The main inspiration could be Mick's girlfriend at the time, who was also the subject of "I'm So Bored with You," that early version of "I'm So Bored with the U.S.A.," or simply a generic tale about a girl. As things develop through the lyric, we hear a reference to the 100 Club, a tiny rock venue that supported punk early on and that now is famed at a level on par with The Roxy for helping to ignite the scene. It seems the girl lamented in the lyric was invited to the club, declined, but then showed up alone. Later, it appears she's prostituting herself to keep pace with her habit.

OPPOSITE: Backstage at the Royal College of Art, London, November 5, 1976. "Deny" was one of Mick's pre-Clash songs. Was it a veiled message to early Clash member Keith Levene or more simply a boy/girl tale with a dark edge?

ABOVE: *Sounds* advert for the July 17, 1977, Rag Market punk festival in Birmingham.

Critics have noted the similarity of vocal phrasing to the Sex Pistols song "Liar," which Mick had heard from Pistols bassist Glen Matlock. Another interesting feature is the fade-in to start the song. Mick has also remarked that some of the concluding bits were written by the Pretenders' Chrissie Hynde, who was now part of the London scene, having relocated from her native Ohio and jammed with Mick at his nan's tower block flat in the early months of 1976.

The *what a liar* backing vocal all over this closing jam (and attendant Strummer ad-lib) was performed by Mick and Paul, the latter of which later commented on how out of breath they got putting down the take.

Not a live favorite, "Deny" was played in the early days and then essentially shelved after the White Riot Tour in May 1977. Of note, however, is the fact that one night the band changed *what a liar* to *what a Norman* in tribute to the band's disciplinarian tour bus driver.

LONDON'S BURNING

STRUMMER/JONES 2:10

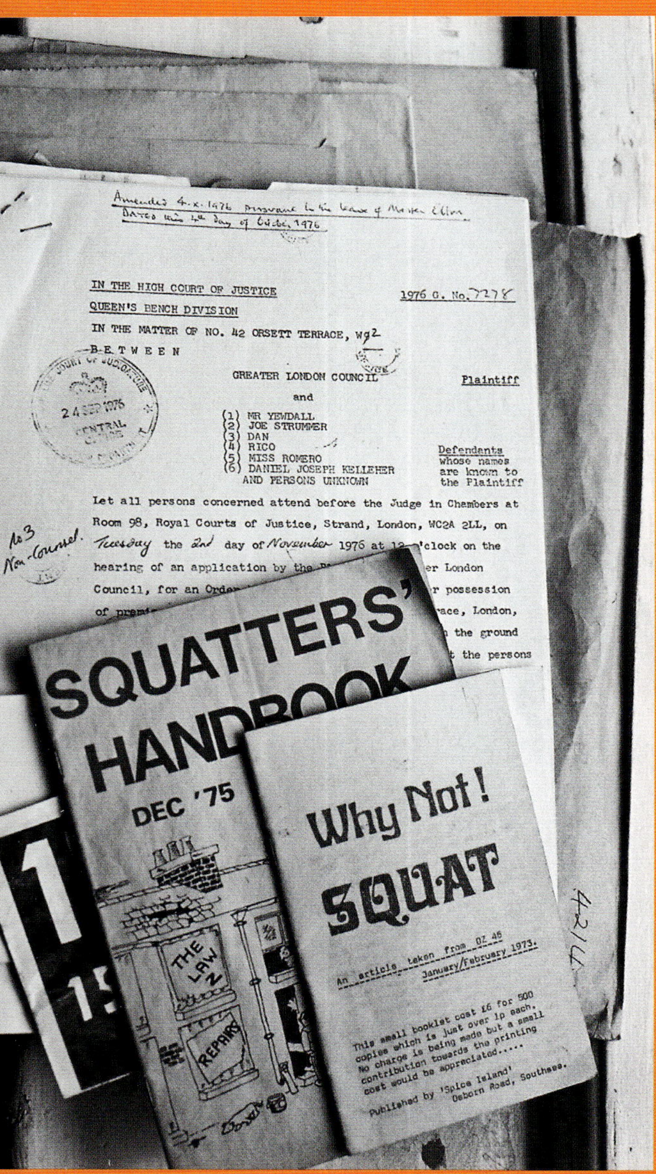

Call this one a take on the popular nursery rhyme of the same name concerning the five-day Great Fire of London in 1666, only updated for 1977. Now London is burning with the headlights of cars stuck in traffic, streetlights, the anesthetizing glow of television, and ultimately boredom. But boredom is a call to action, and it is said that the reference to "speeding around underneath the yellow lights" suggests one antidote, namely, speed or amphetamine sulfate, which the band used to keep themselves functioning at high velocity.

In the third verse, Joe goes into detail about squatting, a big part of his desperate survivalist lifestyle back to his 101ers days when he fancied himself a reincarnation of Woody Guthrie, in fact calling himself Woody and eager to kill fascists with his guitar. When he says he's "in the subway," he isn't referring to a train but the underground walkways beneath London leading to abandoned blocks and Victorian houses ripe for anarchist living.

Joe recalled penning the track at yet another squat, the top floor at 42 Dorset Terrace shared with Keith Levene, Paul Simonon, and even Sid Vicious. Joe said he wrote it very quietly because his then-girlfriend, Palmolive of pioneering female punk band the Slits, was asleep in the room. The actual vantage point that inspired the song's musings about a civilization stuck at night was the eighteenth floor of the West London tower block where Mick lived with his grandmother and where much songwriting took place.

In "London's Burning" Joe provides some detail about squatting. These squatters' handbooks are accompanied by a 1976 document giving notice of a court hearing regarding a squat occupied by Joe in 1976. Prior to the final eviction, Clash bassist Paul and Sid Vicious also lived at the address.

The jaunty, choppy, and even poppy musical track is congruent with imagery of the lyrics, with Joe stabbing the title words in unison with the opening chords before Mick and Paul join in for the almost celebratory chorus about their city on fire. There's not much to the music, although Mick turns in one of his typically traditional rock 'n' rolling freight train guitar solos during the outro over a dramatic key change, while Chimes distinguishes his part with repeated flams on snare. Bottom line, the song serves as another chapter in the story of *The Clash* as a concept album about a society that no longer cuts it for bored teenagers.

It is notable that "London's Burning" was one of five topically entwined tracks chosen for recording in November 1976 in a demo session at Polydor Studios, Oxford Street, with the notorious Guy Stevens producing, though it was Polydor engineers Vic Smith and Chris Perry who wrestled the band's performances onto tape (Stevens would later return as nominal producer of *London Calling*). The demo rendition of "London's Burning" lacks the energy of the LP take, and the guitar sound is positively archaic. The session was set up as an audition of sorts, and of course the band eventually signed with CBS after that label offered them a larger advance.

Amusingly, Joe later said that in using "London's Burning" to audition hopefuls to replace Terry Chimes, the band grew sick of the song after playing it with "two hundred drummers."

The Clash followed the spring 1977 White Riot Tour with autumn's Out of Control Tour, featuring support from former Television and Heartbreakers bassist Richard Hell and his Voidoids.

Beneath the London Westway, the elevated freeway mentioned in "London's Burning."

JANIE
JONES
DON'T

CAREER OPPORTUNITIES

STRUMMER/JONES 1:51

With UK unemployment rates in the 5 percent range throughout the late 1970s under Jim Callaghan and the Labour Party (although, granted, rising as of 1977), it would seem that career opportunities shouldn't have been much of an issue to Strummer. But Joe's lament in this track (title courtesy of Simonon, who nicked it from a piece he read in the *Evening Standard*) is more about the *kind* of jobs available at the time, as well as those suggested by guidance counselors when he was younger, namely menial, body-breaking, soul-sucking, dead-end jobs—nothing for a punk who wants a white riot of his own.

Strummer hollers a laundry list of the jobs from which he'd run the other way, including making tea at the BBC, cop, the RAF, the army, the civil service, bus driver, ambulance man, and ticket inspector. Most humorous is opening letter bombs, a nod to Mick's brief tenure with the long-defunct Department of Health and Social Security, where he was assigned by his seniors to open packages to make sure they didn't contain surprises from the IRA.

By the end of the song, Joe is warning that they're going to have to draft him to make him work, although there's a sense that, as in "White Riot" and "What's My Name," he's got little choice in the matter; in the end most youth of the period, punk or not, will be absorbed by the system. There's also the inference that a cynical establishment sends kids to work for no other reason than to keep them out of jail. But there's more to it—The Clash are not suggesting left-wing opposition to a right-wing work ethic but rather a world beyond work.

"Career Opportunities," banged together at the rehearsal space in a half hour according to Mick, is one of The Clash's first-rate anthems, with Joe's aggression matched to a heavy punk track that retains melody without lapsing into pop, somewhat in the spirit of The Who at their most heroic. As in "Janie Jones" and "Remote Control," exercises in military rhythmic unison separate the verses, the end result being a focused credo atop a persuasive rock 'n' roll track that combined to make the song a live highlight of every Clash show.

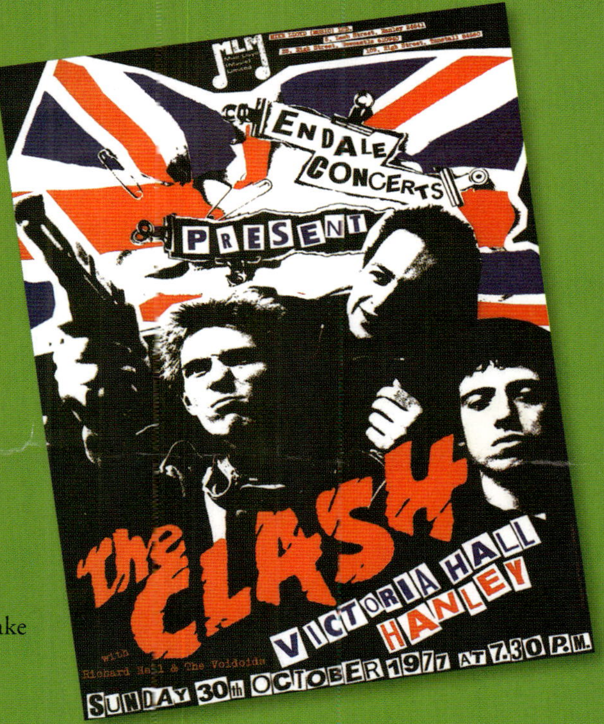

A poster advertising a date on the Out of Control Tour alongside Adrian Boot's original image, taken pre-Topper at the band's Camden rehearsal space.

CHEAT

STRUMMER/JONES 2:06

OPPOSITE: "Cheat" features an enthusiastic chorus that counters punk's frequent defeatist underdog stance with more of a wizened streetwise view. Out of Control Tour, autumn 1977.

BELOW: Poster for the Out on Parole Tour, June 28–July 27, 1978.

Another scowling lyric of cynical personal politics, "Cheat" aligns with "White Riot" and "Hate & War" in painting a picture of the punk less as beaten down and more as a tempered streetwise taker. In that light, it's a contrast to the likes of the more defeatist "What's My Name" and even "Career Opportunities," with all of them together somewhat ironically suggesting the idea of existing without work—ironic because nowhere in any of this do The Clash talk about the fact that they are actually working to carve out their own careers as musicians (let alone as rock stars). The enthusiasm in the song's chorus reinforces this notion that we are to take the idea of a life without work with a grain of salt. A bit of swearing, a reference to speeding (i.e., going silent when "drugged up"), going wild, Friday nights . . . again, The Clash are hammering home imagery of a desperate lifestyle, restlessness, and the trouble that is inevitable.

The song was not played live regularly, and Strummer in fact considered it something of a filler track written late in the process of making the album and thus never played live before it was cut. Furthermore, it wouldn't make the grade when the eponymous debut was reconfigured for US release in 1979.

In terms of musical style, "Cheat" is nevertheless a good fit on the record—short, pointy, punky, and perfect for Joe's slashing down strokes as the band's rhythm guitarist. An odd touch is the phase-shifter effect added by engineer Simon Humphrey, on Bernie's and Mick's instruction, as an homage to The Small Faces' "Itchycoo Park."

PROTEX BLUE

STRUMMER/JONES 1:45

Another of the quirky songs Mick wrote back when London SS was threatening to become a real band and, in fact, even before Mick met Paul, "Protex Blue" is a quick and panicky hard rocker that fits musically with the spirit of the album's short, hard-hitting, melodic songs, many of which predict the post-punk future, in this case wiry Gang of Four–like guitar scratched out by Joe at the intro. Once it kicks in, the rhythm guitars panned hard left and hard right play subtly different rhythms and harmonies, creating a nice weave similar in theory to the trademark styles of AC/DC and the Stones. Simonon and Chimes are recorded particularly clearly, accentuating their tightness as a rhythm section despite Paul's novice status.

Lyrically, the song is an adolescent paean to condoms, Protex Blue being a brand commonly stocked in vending machines at the time, a fact referenced at the outset with the mention of buying one in the "bog" (i.e., lavatory) of a pub. Of course, there's also the question of whether or not it will get used in any fumbling encounter, as well as reflections on its usefulness for a clean solo encounter after a long commute. The narrator's various marvels at the ingenuity of the device is celebrated at the close with a spirited *Johnny, Johnny*! (*Johnny* being slang for condom).

Building on references in other songs on the record, "Protex Blue" reinforces the experiences of the band in West London, with the opening lines "Standing in the bog of a West End bar" and "Sitting in the carriage of a Bakerloo," or a subway car on one of the lines serving the West End.

Although not a set regular, "Protex Blue" bears the distinction of being the first song the band ever played live. Early renditions were performed at a frantic pace, but by the time of its occasional appearances on set lists in 1979 and into 1980, the tempo had reverted to match that of the studio original.

OPPOSITE: Paul and Terry are recorded particularly clearly on "Protex Blue," accentuating their tightness as a rhythm section. Out of Control Tour, autumn 1977.

POLICE & THIEVES

LEE PERRY/JNR.MURVIN 6:00

White Riot Tour, the Electric Circus, Manchester, England, May 8, 1977.

Predicting their status as deft and enthusiastic practitioners of reggae, The Clash go left field before the paint on the punk is even dry, whipping up a cover that's also the longest, jammiest song by far on their debut—and the biggest outlier to boot.

Junior Murvin, a minor reggae artist from Jamaica, had recorded "Police and Thieves" (no ampersand) the previous year, with legendary Lee "Scratch" Perry producing. First released as a single in Jamaica and then by Island Records in the UK, the song became associated with the 1976 Notting Hill riots, making it little surprise the song came to the band's attention as they assembled their debut. The band added the odd bit of color commentary, but the most interesting nuance carried forward from the original is the focus on thieves and the point that as much grief is caused by outlaws as by police.

The Clash had no plans to include "Police & Thieves" on the album until they were jamming it one day at rehearsals and decided to go for it, calling their version "punk reggae." Murvin's version was a slow drip,

Sort It Out Tour, Paris, October 16, 1978.

traditional psychedelic reggae topped with his distinct falsetto delivery that intimidated the hell out of Joe as he tried to figure out a way to make his approach. His yobbish bark is galaxies from Murvin's style, lending a bit of menace until the slightly more urgent and hard rock pre-chorus (which doesn't lead to a chorus per se). Building a bridge to the original, Mick adds falsetto "Oh yeah" responses. Upon hearing the treatment, Murvin was said to have remarked, "They have destroyed Jah work!" Perry was none too pleased either.

Already well-versed in reggae politics, Joe and Mick played stabbing and accentuated reggae rhythms all over *The Clash*, albeit within the songs' punk contexts. As for Mick's lead guitar performance, well, his first solo is dead simple and therefore inexcusable in its clumsiness, but his second go-round finds him in a fine two-string rock 'n' roll mode, blurring the line between solo and rhythm part, jamming, texturizing, helping extend the song way past usual Clash standards before an uncharacteristic fadeout.

The call-and-response rhythm guitars (panned hard left and hard right); Paul's tight, articulated, front-and-center bass line (he was the band's biggest reggae fan, in fact); and the general architecture, rife with space, all combine to make "Police & Thieves" eminently more accessible than the original and create a rock-reggae blueprint that The Police would later take to the bank on weekly trips.

Lest The Clash stray too far from punk, Joe throws in "They're going through a tight wind" (possibly saying "We're") as a bonus opening line, which also happens to be an early line in the Ramones' "Blitzkrieg Bop," a hit song on one of arguably the only two punk albums to precede *The Clash*.

48 HOURS

STRUMMER/JONES 1:34

In the true spirit of filler, "48 Hours" was knocked together in a half hour upstairs in the rehearsal spot because, Mick claimed, the band needed another track to help make the album long enough. A purpose is served, the song being another to add to the half-dozen or so pert punk rockers on *The Clash*, jumpy yet melodic, rife with quick transitions, distinguished somewhat by Chimes's drum work, who, across three movements, goes from no high-hat to eighth notes to quarter notes. As if to betray the song as a lark, Joe's solo—his only true lead on a Clash song—is a train wreck of post-punk noisemaking, made the more jarring by its placement way up in the mix.

Lyrically, the band is back to discussing the weekend, Strummer all revved up with nothing to do, almost tormented with a desperation to fill all forty-eight hours with "forty-eight thrills"—in fact "Cheap thrills/Any kind of thrill." "London's Burning," "What's My Name?" "Protex Blue," "Janie Jones," "Career Opportunities"—all are essentially about boredom. Here the most poetic line reads, "Monday is coming like a jail on wheels."

Rock Against Racism, Victoria Park, London, April 30, 1978. Some 100,000 marched to the East End park for the show organized in response to a rash of racist attacks in the UK. Sham 69, Generation X, and Steel Pulse were among other bands on the bill.

GARAGELAND

STRUMMER/JONES 3:13

The last track on the album was written as a response to a negative review by Charles Shaar Murray, who in August 1976 called The Clash a garage band that should essentially go back to the garage, close the door, and leave the engine running.

After addressing the review in the first verse ("Carbon monoxide making sure it's effective/People ringing up making offers for my life"), Joe counters that the band is proud to be a garage band, proud to be from "garageland," and that they weren't about to buy new boots or wear suits (perhaps a reference to The Jam) or hang out with the rich, whether they were label execs or band buddies suddenly on fat contracts now that punk was becoming a business (granted, The Clash weren't doing too badly themselves). According to Paul, the line *Complaints! Complaints! Wot an old bag* is about a woman who complained about the noise when the band practiced at their Davies Road squat.

The verse rhythm plods somewhere between a march and shuffle before the band breaks into their by now familiar angular punctuations glazed with ethereal "Aah-aah-aah" backing vocals. Mick's harmonica washes and some particularly choral, reverb-drenched guitar give the song texture beyond the norm; the back third gets a whole new part, propelled by Chimes's snare and tom-tom rolls. It's a fitting windup to the album, the overall effect being that of revisiting the terrace chant vibe presented time and time again on *The Clash*—even though punk and football at the time had absolutely nothing to do with each other.

Hanging from the rafters at the Rafter Club. Out on Parole Tour, Manchester, England, July 3, 1978.

IN THE SHOPS

NEW SINGLE

CLASH

JAIL
GUITAR
DOORS

802
DYE

SINGLES GOING STEADY

THE CLASH REPURPOSED FOR AMERICA

The relatively tidy Clash catalog sure didn't start that way, relations with CBS getting off on a bad foot when the label refused to release *The Clash* in the all-important American market due to what they considered its crude production. So instead of riding the punk wave (the album nevertheless sold 100,000 units in the United States as an import), the label sat this one out, much to the chagrin of the band and Bernard Rhodes.

As a result, The Clash's first US release would be *Give 'Em Enough Rope*, issued on November 10, 1978, with an altered version of *The Clash* finally showing up on American shelves on July 26, 1979.

To convince the most dedicated US punks to buy the record twice—and to make it more palatable for American tastes—CBS came up with a smart set of song swaps. Gone from the US version were "Deny," "Cheat," "Protex Blue," and "48 Hours," arguably the weakest and least lyrically ideological tracks on the original UK issue and not the strongest musically either. CBS (subsidiary Epic Records in the states) also switched out the album version of "White Riot" for the original pre-LP single version, helping underscore the redo's singles-friendly theme.

With respect to the American additions, CBS didn't have to scrape the barrel for unreleased tracks, given that The Clash had been busy like good punks, putting out flash non-LP singles throughout the balance of 1977 and into 1978. These songs—four A-sides, a B-side, and an EP track—would transform the UK debut into a vastly different package and the only version most Americans would know until the age of CD reissues and repackages.

COMPLETE CONTROL

STRUMMER/JONES/3:12

The first of the singles added to the US version was an A-side from September 23, 1977, a rough and rowdy old-time rocker that tells the story of the label issuing "Remote Control" as a single against the band's wishes (see pages 16–17). Amusingly, on the US edition, the label sequenced it right after "Remote Control."

Lyrically, this one is all Mick, who recalled writing the song in his Wilmcote house bedroom. CBS isn't the only target of his ire—so is Bernie Rhodes, who had assumed much control over the band, the biggest sting being his 20 percent take of the Clash's initial £100,000 advance, and his 20 percent after that being calculated *before* expenses. However, the impetus for writing the song was more amusing than all that, with the title stemming from an incident outside a pub in which Rhodes declared, "I want complete control!"

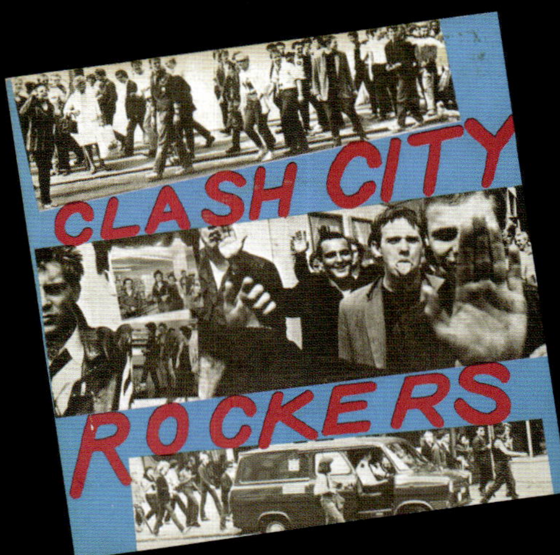

CLASH CITY ROCKERS

STRUMMER/JONES/3:55

The band had issued "Clash City Rockers" backed with "Jail Guitar Doors" on February 17, 1978. The A-side is a surprisingly garage-y spot of "I Can't Explain" punk, recorded rough and raw, save for a token keyboard line, with Joe shouting hoarsely like it's still late 1976 amid British punk's infancy. Still, a sense of indulgence places it squarely within the mien of *Give 'Em Enough Rope*, especially its slightly psychedelic closing movement and the fact that at four minutes it was the band's longest original to date. Lyrically, the song was inspired by Rockers, as in the West Indian reggae genre. Also, its critique of '70s rock stars—Gary Glitter, David Bowie—and its mention of Jamaican DJ and producer Prince Far I are quite telling.

JAIL GUITAR DOORS

STRUMMER/JONES/3:05

"Jail Guitar Doors," the B-side to "Clash City Rockers," is a gorgeous, groovy, sumptuously recorded, Stones-styled rocker that can compete with anything on *Give 'Em Enough Rope* for that magical sense of heroism The Clash could confer. The guitars are huge, Topper brings the big beat (using a bent high-hat in the treated intro), and Mick sings his heart out, offering tribute to Fleetwood Mac founder Peter Green, Keith Richards, and MC5's Wayne Kramer and their respective jail times over a melody nicked from The 101ers. Mick's riff is done with a bottleneck—a little-known Clash fact!

WHITE MAN IN HAMMERSMITH PALAIS

STRUMMER/JONES/3:58

Helping "Police & Thieves" seem less the outlier on the US issue was reggae Clash original "White Man in Hammersmith Palais," an ambitious, name-dropping yet melodic pure reggae laden with production (including piano, wood block, and vocal and guitar effects) and timing fairly long at nearly four minutes. Lyrically, this is Joe at his most substantial and dense yet, attacking the complexity of reggae culture politics and the commercialization of punk and then managing to tie the two together.

I FOUGHT THE LAW

S. CURTIS/2:40

The Clash turned in a spirited, punk-heroic version of the rock 'n' roller written by Sonny Curtis and made famous by the Bobby Fuller Four. The band had heard it on the studio jukebox in San Francisco when doing overdubs for *Give 'Em Enough Rope*, thus becoming happily reacquainted with the English pub rock staple and eventually making their studio recording of it, the first track on a UK-only five-track EP called *The Cost of Living*.

Early copies of *The Clash* in the United States included a bonus 7-inch containing "Groovy Times" backed with "Gates of the West" (also from *The Cost of Living*), both astonishing and forward-thinking songs that essentially leap the clanging guitars of *Give 'Em Enough Rope*, aiming directly at the world-beating Clash of *London Calling*. This 7-inch was also available in Canada, where, given that the original UK version of the LP had already been issued back in 1977, Epic changed the cover's green to navy blue and issued the album a second time, now with the US track selections. One might surmise that the success of the US edition of *The Clash* represents a rare case where the exercise of "complete control" by a record label worked out fortuitously for all parties.

THE CLA
GIVE 'EM ENOUGH RO

SIDE 1

SAFE EUROPEAN HOME

ENGLISH CIVIL WAR

TOMMY GUN

JULIE'S BEEN WORKING
FOR THE DRUG SQUAD

LAST GANG IN TOWN

SIDE 2

GUNS ON THE ROOF

DRUG-STABBING TIME

STAY FREE

CHEAPSKATES

ALL THE YOUNG PUNKS
(NEW BOOTS AND
CONTRACTS)

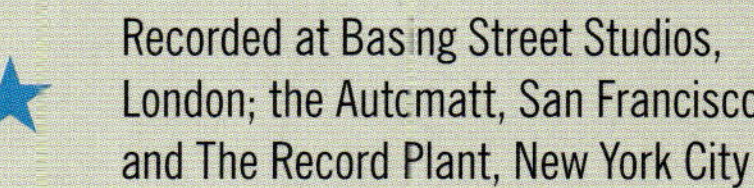

Recorded at Basing Street Studios, London; the Autcmatt, San Francisco; and The Record Plant, New York City

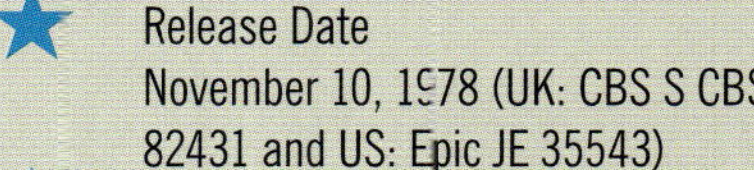

Release Date
November 10, 1978 (UK: CBS S CBS 82431 and US: Epic JE 35543)

Produced by Sandy Pearlman
Engineered by Dennis Ferranti, Gregg Caruso, Kevin Dalimore, and Chris Mingo
Recorded and mixed by Corky Stasiak

RIAA Certification: n/a
Top *Billboard* Position: No. 128

GIVE 'EM ENOUGH ROPE

JOE STRUMMER
Lead and Backing Vocals,
Rhythm Guitar

MICK JONES
Lead and Backing Vocals,
Lead Guitar

PAUL SIMONON
Bass, Backing Vocals

TOPPER HEADON
Drums

GUESTS:
Allen Lanier, Piano
Stan Bronstein, Saxophone
Bob Andrews, Keyboards

Since the day it was released, Clash fans and onlookers with brains and perhaps even some skin in the game have been tied up in knots, as it were, about *Give 'Em Enough Rope.* The record has always been overshadowed by the band's flamethrower of a debut, by the spate of impressive non-LP singles leading up to the clumsy release of *Rope*, and by the majesty of *London Calling.*

Another spanner in the works has always been the unlikely choice of a producer, Sandy Pearlman, whose pedigree was never considered punk enough for the band. Plus, he was American to boot, perking the antennae of Brits always touchy about bands selling out, leaving home, abandoning their ideals, or even forgetting to book a UK leg of their next tour due to tax issues and other lofty rock star concerns.

Even though history wrings its hands, *Give 'Em Enough Rope* was well received at the time, and let's remember, it was the first Clash album released in America, which meant it generated a lot of talk and serious debate.

The cover is of a roughshod proto-hardcore design, and the music is similarly and inspiringly heavy and guitar-charged punk for the time, late 1978, when punk was already all but dead . . . the UK had by then become a post-punk world, elitist and artsy, and America had pretty much moved on (Dead Boys who?) straight into a more benign version of the original idea known as new wave, soon to cough up the Cars and The Knack and switch out the Ramones for Blondie and Talking Heads down on the Lower East Side.

Into this environment parachuted a new Clash record representing, albeit subtly, a new Clash. One key difference is the fact that *Give 'Em Enough Rope* has longer songs (and fewer: ten this time versus fourteen on the debut) averaging a previously unimaginable three-and-a-half minutes per song. But given the talents of The Clash, every precious additional second produces much inspiring rock 'n' roll guitar-banging and sloganeering, to the point where one must consider *Give 'Em Enough Rope* for the title of Greatest Clash Album of All Time.

Of course that's crazy, especially given the later release of the towering *London Calling.* Just as in a parlor game, we could

handicap the double album. On second thought, let's not go there. Sanity must prevail as we all settle into the fact that *London Calling* is, in many a smart listener's estimation, one of the greatest half-dozen or so albums of all time—double or not.

Better to discuss what The Clash managed to accomplish with this flamethrower of an album at a time when, for so many, the ideals had died, old punks staring backward, hungover, like their hippie predecessors in 1972. Fact is that *Give 'Em Enough Rope* represented a raging against the dying of the light, or at minimum an action against insipid commercialism. So rather than sneer at its often smothering heaviness and Joe-croaked bluntness, we should celebrate that The Clash beat us black and blue in 1978 when outside of this crucible of rock-hard hope, punk was dying. In other words, American production or not, The Clash were still extolling the virtues of traditional thrashing against a turning tide. And for that we should look less askance at the hype surrounding the band and focus on the sincere motivations of a gang besieged and rising, fangs exposed, to the challenge befalling them.

The band in New York City, October 1978. Joe and Mick were returning from work on the album in California and met up with Paul and Topper in the Big Apple. The city would later play a significant role in their career.

SAFE EUROPEAN HOME

STRUMMER/JONES 3:49

OPPOSITE: New York calling . . .

One could compare the musical volley that opens *Give 'Em Enough Rope* to explosions, mortar fire, or snipers on a roof. Drummer Topper Headon is responsible for the gunplay, opening the record with a lone snare shot before the band collapses into the fat chords layered over the fatter groove of "Safe European Home." Mick is still a Les Paul man here, but Joe's Telecaster was busted for a time, so he took to playing a Gibson ES-345 hollowbody for much of the *Rope* sessions. Whether that's the cause or not (producer Sandy Pearlman deserves much of the credit as well), The Clash arrive at a muscle rock sound to match their hollering and bitter politicking.

"Safe European Home" tells the story of a ten-day writing trip, apparently at Bernie's suggestion, that Mick and Joe took to Jamaica in November 1977 to come up with songs for the second album. (Paul, the band's biggest reggae fan, was furious he didn't get to go.) True to the band's sense of lyrical sophistication, they don't glamorize or idealize the trip but rather express that they felt endangered in Jamaica, even ripe for the picking as white guys hanging around the harbor buying weed. It didn't help that Jamaica was essentially undergoing a civil war at the time.

Even so, the longing for a safe European home sounds a little forced here, as if what Joe is really saying is, "Look, get out of your comfort zone and see the world." This theory is underscored by the fact Strummer extolls of the virtues of the trip, referencing natty dread (Rastas) drinking at the Sheraton, bluebeat music, rude boys who can't fail, Jamaican crime classic *The Harder They Come*, sun, palm trees, and, of course, weed. Despite the trip somewhat backfiring (including Joe and Mick not being able to find legendary musician and producer Lee "Scratch" Perry, the only guy they knew on the island), the pair did manage to write "Safe European Home" and a few other songs while working at the Pegasus Hotel in Kingston.

Musically speaking, "Safe European Home" is a confident rocker, and the closing jam finds them honing their concept of punk reggae, with counterpoint slashing chords over a bouncy rhythm bed topped with surround-sound vocals and a magical false ending. With the first track on the new record, suggestions that The Clash were larger than life begin to make sense.

ENGLISH CIVIL WAR

TRAD. ARR. STRUMMER/JONES 2:49

The traditional Irish song "Johnny I Hardly Knew Ye" and the more famed "When Johnny Comes Marching Home," beloved by both sides in the American Civil War, are the sources for this bleak call to arms nearly verging on heavy metal.

The inference is that, in 1978, an English Civil War didn't seem entirely out of the question and that when Johnny does come marching home, it will be a trip he can make on public transit—a wry bit of silver lining. Equally chilling is the realism of beatings described that reflect the sectarian violence already a reality in Britain, much of it race-based and carried out by the skinheads and the National Front, who were at their peak in the mid-'70s and threatening to become a political presence. Joe draws parallels to the fascist New Party of the 1930s, suggesting history could repeat itself. The Clash, ever willing to speak out, debuted the song live at an Anti-Nazi League rally in April 1978.

The band does not relent after the explosive blast of "Safe European Home." "English Civil War" receives an incendiary performance, Joe venomous and ominous with his punk holler, Mick firing off greasy, low-slung licks and soloing twice, spurred on by the raucous Topper.

"English Civil War" was issued as a UK single on February 23, 1979, reaching No. 25 in the charts. Adding a layer of meaning, the picture sleeve features a scene from an animated version of George Orwell's *Animal Farm*, produced by John Halas in 1954. The suggestion is that civil war often ends badly, with the rise of a strongman and the attendant ruthless stifling of freedoms, all the more salient given that freedom—political, economic, personal—was ultimately The Clash's favorite cause.

OPPOSITE: Strummer outside Cinema Blue in Soho, London, following a press reception for *Give 'Em Enough Rope*, November 2, 1978.

RIGHT: The "English Civil War" art uses a still from the 1954 animated adaption of George Orwell's dystopian novella, *Animal Farm*.

TOMMY GUN

STRUMMER/JONES 3:14

ABOVE: "Tommy Gun" b/w "1-2 Crush on You," UK, November 24, 1979.

OPPOSITE: Pearl Harbour Tour, Geary Temple, San Francisco, February 8, 1979. The short nine-date tour marked the band's first performances on US soil.

Recalling the structure of "Remote Control," "Janie Jones," and "London's Burning," "Tommy Gun" opens with a rhythmic exercise, in this case Topper executing single-stroke rolls that sound like automatic weapon discharge, before the band collapses into the verses' hanging chords.

But the band has surprises in store, with the beat dropping out for the second verse (and again later) and the lyrics essentially dropping out for a "verse" in which Joe sings "Tommy gun" followed by Mick in languished solo mode. Essentially the song has no chorus, but as with other Clash songs, it offers a pre-chorus as well as a closing tour de force of completely different modulated construction, presaged by a solo section where Mick chimes on a repeating high note.

Lyrically, Joe makes the point that terrorists enjoy their own press as much as rock stars and that the perceived glory of their exploits only breeds more terrorists. The most overt reference is to the Palestinian conflict, but to add shade, Joe spoke in the press at the time about understanding the Palestinian plight against Israel. Further dimension comes from a reading of Tommy Gun as a person, which suggests a mercenary.

"Tommy Gun" was issued in the United Kingdom as a picture sleeve single (the cover of which is a page from a newspaper in Arabic) backed with the non-LP "1-2 Crush on You," managing No. 19 on the UK charts, the band's first Top 20. "Tommy Gun" (along with "Last Gang in Town") debuted live during a three-night stand at the Rainbow in London in mid-December 1977, well before the release of the album, and remained in the set for most of the band's shows.

The song was also the subject of an official video, filmed at a soundcheck before a gig at the Roxy cinema in Harlsden, northwest London, in October 1978. Nothing more than a faux live clip, the camera work nonetheless reinforces the punchiness of the song, emphasizing Topper's snare drum windups. Underscoring the band's forceful politicking, they're filmed playing in front of the band's Sort It Out Tour backdrop of national flags. As well, Joe wears an H-Block T-shirt, expressing solidarity with IRA prisoners who rioted in the spring of 1978. The shirt caused some controversy, as did other stage gear and press statements that appeared to express sympathy for Italy's Red Brigade and Germany's Red Army Faction, both far-left organizations. In fact, it has been conjectured that Joe wrote "Tommy Gun" to clarify that he was against the use of violence as a means of achieving political aims.

IGNORE
ALIEN
ORDERS

Gibson

JULIE'S BEEN WORKING FOR THE DRUG SQUAD

STRUMMER/JONES 3:00

A change of pace both musically and lyrically, "Julie's Been Working for the Drug Squad" ("Julie's in the Drug Squad" on some early pressings) finds The Clash adding to a stylistic repertoire that would expand impressively one album hence. Essentially a jaunty barrelhouse blues, the band's performance is augmented almost shockingly by the honky-tonk piano work of Blue Öyster Cult's Allen Lanier, the connection made by producer Sandy Pearlman, who had been BÖC's manager and conceptualist since the beginning. At The Record Plant in New York Pearlman asked Lanier to replace parts first tracked by sixty-year-old New York pianist Al Field. Mick and Joe were somewhat amused by Pearlman's use of session musicians but also concerned that he was trying to turn the band into Fleetwood Mac.

ABOVE: "Tommy Gun" b/w "1-2 Crush on You," UK promo copy.

OPPOSITE: Pearl Harbour Tour, Geary Temple, San Francisco, February 8, 1979.

Topper finally gets to use his jazz and swing training on the track, whose bounciness lends an almost comical, trivial vibe to the story related in the lyric, namely that of a complicated and major UK drug bust instigated in 1975 called Operation Julie (named for one of the many officers on the team). As the opening reference to "Lucy in the Sky with Diamonds" suggests, the drug involved was LSD, the total haul being enough to create 6.5 million tabs with a street value at the time of £100 million—more than £500 million pounds in today's currency. The dragnet resulted in 87 houses being searched, 120 people charged across the United Kingdom and France, and £800,000 found in Swiss bank accounts. In a nice turn of phrase, Strummer notes the cops "took eighty-two laws through eighty-two doors." Again, the nature of the music, coupled with the light telling of the tale, creates a sense of gloating or at least amused marvel at how the bust stuffed the jails full and how all the folks nabbed were going to be locked up for a long time for their psychedelic folly.

In the opening sequence, and indeed the title, Joe uses up real estate on the idea that the undercover cops, specifically Julie herself, had to partake of LSD to maintain their cover. Elsewhere there are references to true events from the nearly three-year operation. Besides Julie, the main character in real life and in the song is chemist Richard Kemp, who had synthesized the drug in the United Kingdom beginning in 1969. The line about "someone looking down/From that mountainside" refers to the authorities surveilling Kemp's Welsh cottage from a farmhouse (Joe lived in Wales around that time), including Sgt. Julie Taylor, namesake of the operation. Later in the song, Joe muses that one of the prisoners could have been a physicist.

SANDY PEARLMAN'S MANIFEST DESTINY

DICTATORS AND BÖC COLLABORATOR ON WORKING WITH THE CLASH

It's complicated, the late Sandy Pearlman's long history with Blue Öyster Cult, but suffice to say Pearlman was much more than the band's manager and sorta co-producer (along with Murray Krugman). In fact, Pearlman was one of the first actual rock critics, one of its conceptualists, much like Bernie Rhodes and Malcolm McLaren, and the engine behind many of BÖC's lyrics, including the characters and poems that became the 1988 concept/saga album *Imaginos*. Additionally, he managed New York proto-punk heroes the Dictators and Black Sabbath through their first run with Ronnie James Dio. He spent most of his later years as a music professor, lecturer, and guest speaker, before his death in 2016 at the age of seventy-two.

And, of course, he produced The Clash's second album, *Give 'Em Enough Rope*, after deciding that for intellectual reasons, it was something he must do.

"Both punk and heavy metal were a combination of a very modern electric folk music and a very ancient traditional folk music," Pearlman told me back in 2009, "which is basically at the heart of most of the music coming from the British Isles. If you listen to The Clash and listen through the surface of it, that's what a lot of it is.

"One of the reasons I wound up producing The Clash is they loved 'Godzilla' and 'The Reaper,'" said Pearlman, referring to the BÖC songs and emphasizing the ties between metal and punk. "All of the bullshit about me being forced down their throats as a sellout to tailor them to the American market has nothing to do with anything—none of that's true. They liked those records and they also liked the Dictators. They spoke to [Dictators] Andy Shernoff and Scott Kempner, who said, 'He's awesome', and they liked them so they said let's go. They called up Patti Smith, too, and she said, 'He's awesome.'

"Anyway, the reason why I think myself and The Clash—or myself and U2—constituted an interesting pairing is that I really understood where the music was coming from and where the base or basic vocabulary was. And I figured out ways to project this stuff and make it work very well while amplifying its inherent power, putting a new surface on it while having it remain irresistibly powerful and engaging."

As for the final result, the *Give 'Em Enough Rope* album, Pearlman reasserted that at the heart, "It's folk music; while it has a great deal of heavy metal elements, it's British folk music. There's a great deal of heavy metal at the surface of it, which at times Mick thought was great and times they were revolted by. And that's what happened—it's very electric. So something like 'Safe European Home' is unimaginable without a studio. I mean, you can go out and play it live, but the whole awesome experience from beginning to end is a function

OPPOSITE: Sandy Pearlman in Denmark, 1978. For intellectual reasons, he decided *Give 'Em Enough Rope* was something he must do.

of being in the studio, of having studio aspects that we had available. And there were a lot of times we had to keep down costs. Even when the budget ran out, I was able to underwrite the completion of the record. But the truth was, for the most part it was easier to make the Clash record than to make Blue Öyster Cult records. And if you have any knowledge of the internal dynamics of The Clash, that's quite a statement. And, man, those guys smoked a lot of pot. Heroic amounts of pot [*laughs*]."

Addressing the politics of the record, Pearlman explained, "England was going down the tubes at the time. The socialist experiment . . . I'm not making a political value judgment, it's just that it was defined in the UK as having failed. I remember The Clash speaking to me later when Margaret Thatcher was elected, saying, 'Well, you'll be happy. We have a fascist regime in England now.' They had a lot of things they were pissed off about and reacted against it. I mean, you would have had to have been in the UK in the mid- to late '70s to appreciate how depleted the society was and how much they had to be mad about. And they expressed it."

Asked whether he was surprised at the abrupt left turn the band would take on *London Calling*, Pearlman said, "No, not at all. I'm surprised by the varying afterlife of *Give 'Em Enough Rope*. I mean Tommy Morello of Rage Against the Machine came up to me about five years ago and said, 'I just want to tell you the first side of *Give 'Em Enough Rope* is the most perfect side of music I've ever heard in my life.' And it is great. I don't listen to the record, but when I finished it I was really happy with it."

The album should have been much more successful, Pearlman said, but for a bad batch of records. "Yes, one of the problems immediately out of the box, a little-known fact, is that Epic decided to distribute the first run of the record, the first 100,000 copies of the LP version, even though there was a defect in the manufacturing. Unlike when the second Led Zeppelin came out and Eddie Kramer had made the loudest sounding record of all time, a record that could not be tracked, right? Atlantic ate many copies of it because they did not want to screw with the career of Led Zeppelin, who were already the biggest band in the world. But in the case of Epic, they thought that it was better just to put out 100,000 lousy-sounding copies of the record than just junk them and come out with a version that actually sounded like the record I made.

"I resent what happened," Pearlman continued, "because given the right circumstances, it is probable that a record that was dominated by the sound of *Give 'Em Enough Rope* would have been the biggest record they ever had. Because it would actually have plugged them into a heavy metal audience—which would have appalled them—but since half of it is heavy metal, it would have plugged the band into that huge, massive, and growing audience. I mean, there are people now who kind of regard a lot of *Give 'Em Enough Rope* as New Wave of British Heavy Metal. And that's the truth! But they were just appalled because they didn't understand that heavy metal was folk music that was authentic. They were embarrassed by it because they saw the NWOBHM as just stupidity. None of that's true! I mean, *all* of that is true, but on the other hand, *none* of it is true [*laughs*]."

OPPOSITE: Sort It Out Tour, Kings Hall, Derby, England, November 24, 1978.

DEREK BLOCK presents
DERBY CITY COUNCIL ENTERTAINMENTS
THE
KING'S HALL - DERBY
CLASH
PLUS SUPPORT
FRIDAY
NOVEMBER
24th
'78
at 8 p.m.
tickets £ 2.25

LAST GANG IN TOWN

STRUMMER/JONES 5:10

BELOW: Last gang at the Tribal Stomp II Festival, Monterey, California, September 8, 1979. The stop was part of their Take the Fifth Tour. Peter Tosh and Joe Ely also appeared.

OPPOSITE: At home in West London, 1979.

Spaghetti western meets the bent chording of "Deny" meets the old-time rock 'n' roll of "Jail Guitar Doors" and "I Fought the Law."

"Last Gang in Town" is a sloppy pocket rocker about all the factions that were running around London and beating each other up at the time. In that regard, it may as well be about the Wild West.

Whether it's the Crops (skinheads), the Spikes (punks), the Quiffs (rockers), or the Stiffs (probably working-class stiffs), they're all at war, says Joe, who's quite nonplussed about it all or perhaps interested in it all from a detached, anthropological point of view.

Musically the guys seem to side with the rockers, "Last Gang in Town" sounding like Eddie Cochran rockabilly with its strong strumming and Keith Richards–like lead lick, falling apart in places but gamely chugging along like an old steam locomotive going uphill.

The song certainly fits the band's modus operandi as framed by Bernie Rhodes, who told them to write about what they knew, to tear a page from their daily lives. But there's an acceptance here, a lightheartedness that we don't get from "English Civil War" or "Tommy Gun," two tracks where conflict gets real. In that respect, "Last Gang in Town" feels closer to "Julie's Been Working for the Drug Squad," Strummer playing walkabout tour guide in his (apparently) safe European home and pointing out some of the bits that are colorful and amusing—at least from a safe distance.

PLAY LOUD

PLAY LOUD

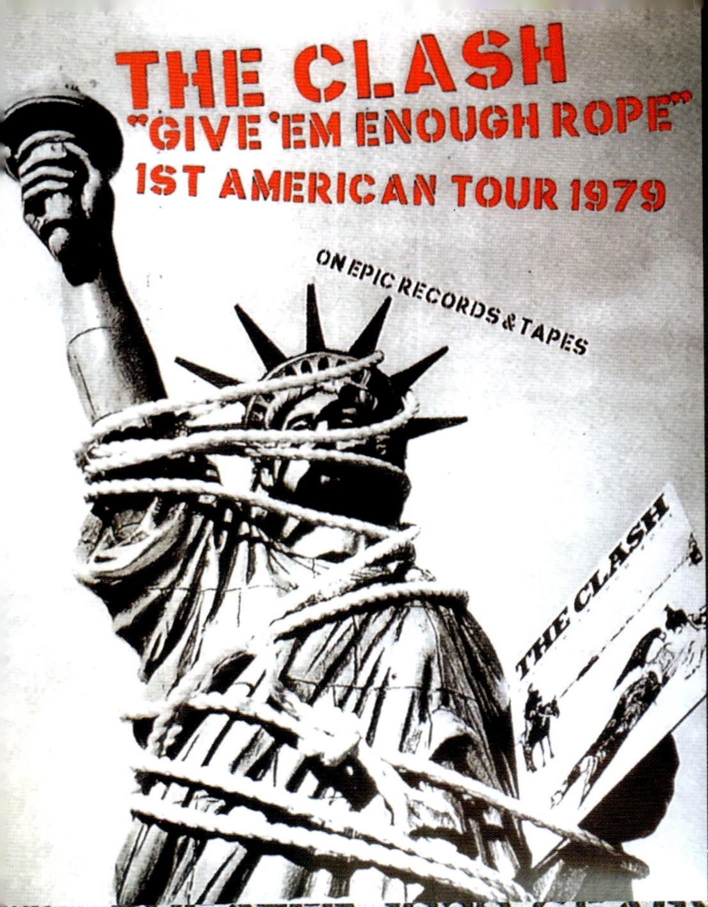

THE CLASH
"GIVE 'EM ENOUGH ROPE"
1ST AMERICAN TOUR 1979
ON EPIC RECORDS & TAPES
THE CLASH

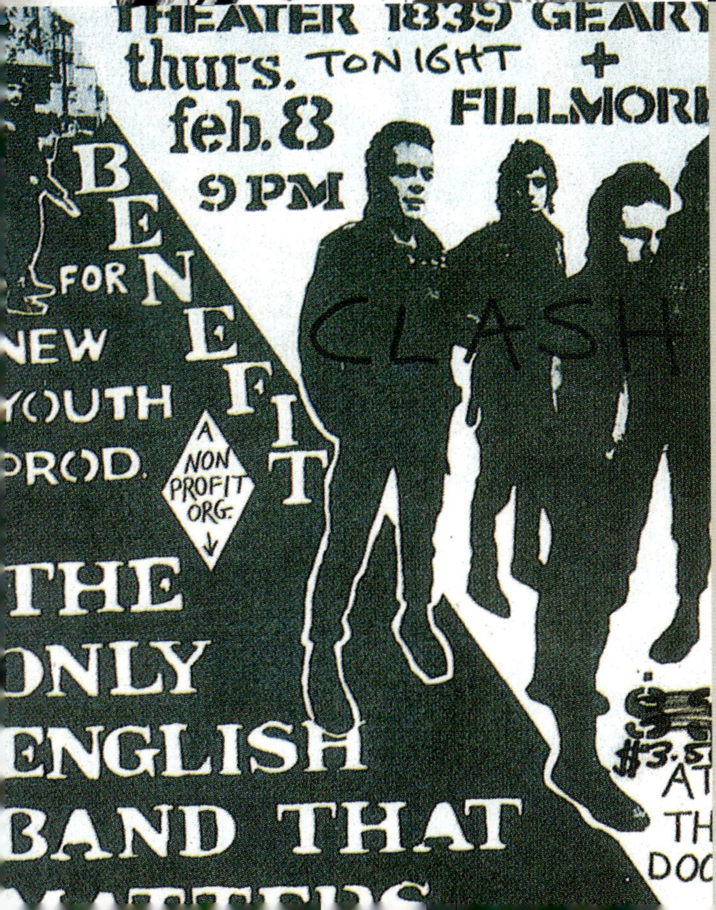

THEATER 1839
thurs. TONIGHT +
feb. 8
9PM
BENEFIT
FOR
A NON PROFIT ORG.
CLASH
THE
ONLY
ENGLISH
BAND THAT

GUNS ON THE ROOF

STRUMMER/JONES/SIMONON/HEADON 3:13

Admittedly built like "Clash City Rocker," upon a rudimentary chord structure straight out of "I Can't Explain," "Guns on the Roof" is a weak link on *Give 'Em Enough Rope*, no thanks to the band's nick an' repeat approach but also due in no small part to its lyrics, which similarly cover old terrain but in a clumsy, sputtering manner.

The song's opening gambit, in which Joe swears himself into court, as well as the title, refer back to a true-life boys-will-be-boys spot of mischief that took place in March '78. Bored as usual waiting for Mick to arrive to the rehearsal space, it was up to the roof with two air pistols and an air rifle. There, a British rail employee spotted Topper, Paul, and Mick's schooldays chum Robin Crocker (and possibly one of the Barnacle brothers from Dover; see "Something About England," page 132) shooting at pigeons, which would scatter and then circle back for more. The rail worker, thinking they were shooting at trains in Euston station, reported the incident but also ventured to the roof with an accomplice and tried to manhandle the guns away from the guys, one of them even hitting Topper hard on the arm with a monkey wrench. All manner of police presence, including eight tactical unit vans and a helicopter, were summoned, the authorities treating the incident as some sort of terrorist attack, given ongoing tensions with the IRA.

Topper and Paul were hauled in, but the charges were later dropped. Further, the pigeons turned out to be trained racing pigeons, which resulted in a payment of £700 to the owner. Other than that, the two got off with fines of £30.

Ultimately "Guns on the Roof" turns out to be a downer, however, with a message of military oppression on one's own populace—a valid concern, perhaps, but badly argued here. Joe's vocal is shouted and sloganeering and the chorus dull. The music across its expanse seems to loiter, fumble a bit, and repeatedly run out of steam due to its internal sequencing, even if Mick's solo is the best on the album. Joe's arguably overselling histrionics on the track caused him to burst a blood vessel in his throat, hence the barely audible "blood in my mouth" at the very end as the amps are cooling.

"Guns on the Roof" is the only track on the album credited not to Joe and Mick but to the whole band. The song was debuted at the Anti-Nazi League event in Victoria Park, London, on April 30, 1978, and it survived in the set through 1979.

OPPOSITE: The Clash hit America for the first time in support of *Give 'Em Enough Rope*—appropriate, given their new American producer and ambitions to transcend English punk.

DRUG-STABBING TIME

STRUMMER/JONES 3:40

Curiously, The Clash saw fit to write up a second story of a drug bust for inclusion on *Rope*, although this one is much smaller in scale. The tale finds an assembly-line working stiff at Ford (already behind the eight ball and paying off a fine) wrecking his family life with heroin and winding up with dodgy friends, one of whom inevitably turns out to be a snitch. His phone gets tapped, and perhaps not surprisingly, his next visitors are more turned-out than the usual, their black shoes "shining and neat."

As throughout the album, the band demonstrates their knack for flash song titling, "Drug-Stabbing Time" advertising itself as much more squalid than it turns out. The song is pointedly and almost impatiently antidrugs. At this point, within the band, Topper wasn't the problem but rather Mick, though in fact The Clash were no saints—cocaine had run a lance through all of the band members to some extent, and Joe had been known to be a heavy drinker for years.

Despite the chaos, Joe and Mick sing much of the vocals together, showing a deft sophistication that also appears with their smartly woven guitar parts.

However, as with "Julie's Been Working for the Drug Squad," the band sets a tale of drug crime to energetic, punked-up party rock, with Topper whacking cowbell quarter notes, an effect that seemed to work well enough, after all, for producer Pearlman and his buddies in Blue Öyster Cult (see "[Don't Fear] The Reaper"). Guest sax player Stan Bronstein from Greenwich Village hippie band Elephant's Memory lends an air of New York to the thing, evoking Billy Joel and Bruce Springsteen (a huge influence on Joe and Mick at the time), even if he's placed a fair way back in the mix. Sandy recorded Bronstein at The Record Plant on West 44th Street, as well as Allen Lanier, who provided piano work on "Julie's Been Working for the Drug Squad." Mick and Joe wound up doing more additional work than expected in both San Francisco and New York, as Topper and Paul were left to cool their heels following the Basing Street sessions that produced most of the tracking for the record.

The band's love of original rock 'n' roll, found in a good half-dozen songs thus far in the catalog, rears up again here, with Mick bringing back those "Last Gang in Town" lead licks as well as passes back and forth into boogie rock, a mortar effect between bricks of modern chording often heard in '70s punk and hard rock (most often in American hard rock). The break seems of casual construction, but soon the band is back to Topper's driving cowbell groove and all is well with the world, with another user locked up and forced to kick cold turkey.

OPPOSITE: "Drug-Stabbing Time" is pointedly antidrugs, though at this point, Topper, whose struggles would later become an issue, wasn't so much the problem as Mick—granted, none in The Clash were saints in this regard.

ABOVE: *The Cost of Living* EP advert, *Melody Maker*, May 26, 1979.

STAY FREE

STRUMMER/JONES 3:36

A gorgeous and novel sort of up-tempo reggae ballad, "Stay Free" finds Mick telling the story of his relationship with childhood chum Robin Crocker. The two had begun their interwoven lives together at Strand Grammar School in South London, with Crocker turning out to be trouble from the start, Mick only a shade less so but fortunately as obsessed with rock 'n' roll as Crocker. Crocker was the first of the pair to learn guitar, even teaching Mick how to tune one for the first time. Mick at least had the long hair and tight pants, dressing the part from tip to toe, and eventually went so far as following Mott the Hoople on tour. Ian Hunter's *Diary of a Rock 'n' Roll Star*, one of rock's early autobiographies, became a sort of template for what Mick aspired to do with his life.

Crocker, however, became a journalist, got laid off, and was then nabbed working as the lookout in the robbery of an off-track betting shop, winding up at Albany Prison on the Isle of Wight for two years. With Crocker out of prison since '75 and hanging out with Jones again, Mick came over to his place one day with an

LEFT: The UK-only five-track EP *The Cost of Living* was released on May 11, 1979, and hinted at the more American-influenced rock to come. Side A features "I Fought the Law" and "Groovy Times"; side B of the original vinyl includes "Gates of the West," "Capital Radio," and "The Cost of Living Advert."

acoustic guitar and played him the song he had written, a sort of wistful autobiography mixed with bits of Crocker's bio, though Mick pointed to the song's universality, saying that it's a common tale.

Crocker recalled he and Mick getting hauled into the office as school kids for arguing over who was better, Chuck Berry or Bo Diddley. In the first verse, Mick pays tribute to school troubles—getting into it with the teachers and classmates. By the second verse, the two find themselves "thrown out" of school. Mick references the Locarno in Streatham (a venue Simonon also fondly recalled from his skinhead past), where he and Crocker used to listen to ska and bluebeat.

Playing pool, getting in fights, smoking menthols . . . Mick moves on to remembering his woodshedding years while Crocker was pulling the job that would land him in prison. Mick goes on to speak of writing to Crocker in jail, asking how hardass the screws (i.e., wardens) were, and then trembling with hope through fragile vocals about how the two would light up the town when Crocker got out.

Mick's sincerity is visceral as he reflects on how happy he was when he heard Crocker was out, and how, even if they couldn't hang out together again, Mick having moved on, he knew Robin would be down at the Crown pub again. He asks Crocker to "have a drink on me" and stay out of trouble. Unfortunately, as Crocker tells it, he wound up incarcerated again in the late '80s after doing a "wages snatch" in Stockholm, robbing a business's payroll that was being delivered from the bank.

Crocker figures into the *Give 'Em Enough Rope* story in a few other instances as well, first for being involved in the "Guns on the Roof" incident (see page 6), but also perhaps more dramatically, for punching producer Sandy Pearlman in the face on their first meeting. Crocker, it turns out, was trying to stop an insistent Pearlman from getting backstage to talk to the band. Legend has it the band paid no mind to the sprawled out Pearlman, stepping over him on the way to the stage and leaving manager Bernie Rhodes to clean up the producer's bloody nose.

"Stay Free," featuring acoustic guitar (rare for the early version of the band) as well as organ by Bob Andrews, keyboardist with Graham Parker and The Rumour, became a live fan favorite and a poignant number for Mick to perform among so many songs featuring lead vocals by Joe.

CHEAPSKATES

STRUMMER/JONES 3:22

On "Cheapskates" the band expresses exasperation toward allegations of selling out. After all, the life of a fledgling rock star isn't all good times.

Back to the Marshalls for The Clash on "Cheapskates," supporting the opinion that, at the time, *Give 'Em Enough Rope* wouldn't have looked out of place in the record collection of an American heavy metal fan. That doesn't mean that the guys had to dumb down their literary side, "Cheapskates" being barbed, colorful, and poetic in turns.

The main point of the lyric is that the band members paid their dues with every menial job imaginable to get to where they were—and that, in fact, where they were was no cakewalk either. You could bet you'd be seeing them down at the launderette.

The sentiment was expressed most pointedly to the press, feeding the notion that the all-powerful English weekly music papers—*Melody Maker*, *NME*, *Sounds*—tended to turn on their own when they saw too much success; here, the lingering news item was the band's signing to a major label for £100,000, most of which was quickly burned up in recording and tour expenses. In the song rock writers are likened to rats on a sinking ship, all complaining about The Clash in unison in order to boost their own street cred and eager to bury this new "establishment" band and ordain the next big thing.

Joe goes on to underscore with exasperation that there's nothing establishment about The Clash, that the life of a fledgling rock star isn't all cocaine and "model girls shedding every stitch." The irony here was that the guys (especially Mick) had nothing against models, and they certainly liked their coke.

The contempt in Joe's voice is matched by the angry near heavy metal of the song's musical frame, Mick filling up every available space with squealing leads and squalls of feedback, even when he's handling the chorus vocal. Topper is raucous as well, particularly in the forceful final verse where the band really throws themselves into it, driving home the point that despite what the weeklies were writing, being thieving cheapskates was the only way for the band to survive.

ALL THE YOUNG PUNKS (NEW BOOTS AND CONTRACTS)

STRUMMER/JONES 4:24

Closing the album with a rock 'n' roll affirmation of identity much like "Garageland" ended the debut, "All the Young Punks (New Boots and Contracts)" finds The Clash making use of a particularly nostalgic-sounding chord progression, much like its namesake inspiration, "All the Young Dudes," the Bowie-penned hit by Mott the Hoople. The title's parenthetical offers a second rock reference, namely the debut album of Ian Dury and the Blockheads, *New Boots and Panties!!*, issued a year previous.

The song carries on somewhat the theme of the track before it, examining the business of being in a band, how far The Clash had come, and how many roadblocks had been put up before them, most notably a management contract that, in a nice turn of phrase, is compared to a mafia contract. Another particularly nice turn of phrase is offered when a wistful Joe recalls telling some "passing yabbos" that they knew how to sing and that they knew how to pose, one of them being Mick with his Les Paul, a "heart attack machine," which recalls the famous "This Machine Kills Fascists" sticker on Woody Guthrie's guitar.

It would have been easy for The Clash to put down the next generation of punks, especially given the cookie-cutter approach bands were taking by mid-1978, but the message is ultimately a hopeful one. Although even The Clash's piece of gold looks like a lump of coal, it's still better for the next wave, "all the young cunts," to persevere. Harsh as that sounds, The Clash's word choice is not as derogatory as it might sound coming from one English punk to another (in England it can simply be taken as slang for "guy")—but how they got away with using the word on record, at that time, is difficult to fathom . . . Alas, give up and the alternative is the factory. "Laugh your life" and "live it now," says Joe.

Winding up the album on a spirited note is a rumbling wall of sound ensemble conclusion o'er which Joe offers one of his great ad-libs, babbling on about forty-five minutes hazy and forty-five minutes crazy, three or four days of this and that and speeding your way through dancing 'til dawn. Or, when not living life at a hundred miles per hour, it's "A spliff, a pound, a half pint of Brown/This is the way we spell Camden Town."

Take the Fifth Tour of America.

The Clash

LONDON

CALLI

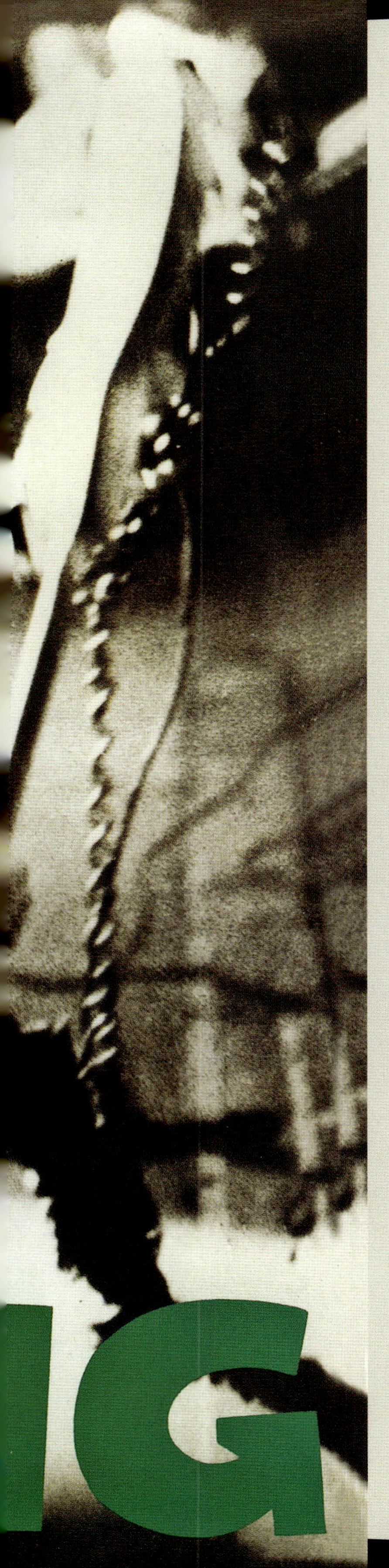

SIDE 1

LONDON CALLING
BRAND NEW CADILLAC
JIMMY JAZZ
HATEFUL
RUDIE CAN'T FAIL

SIDE 2

SPANISH BOMBS
THE RIGHT PROFILE
LOST IN THE SUPERMARKET
CLAMPDOWN
THE GUNS OF BRIXTON

SIDE 3

WRONG 'EM BOYO
DEATH OR GLORY
KOKA KOLA
THE CARD CHEAT

SIDE 4

LOVER'S ROCK
FOUR HORSEMEN
I'M NOT DOWN
REVOLUTION ROCK
TRAIN IN VAIN

Recorded at Wessex Studios, London

Release Dates
December 14, 1979 (UK: S CBS Clash 3)
January 10, 1980 (US: Epic E2 36328)

Produced by Guy Stevens
Engineered by Bill Price (chief engineer) and Jerry Green (second engineer)

RIAA Certification: 1x platinum
Top *Billboard* Position: No. 27

LONDON CALLING

JOE STRUMMER
Vocals, Rhythm Guitar, Piano

MICK JONES
Guitars, Vocals, Harmonica

PAUL SIMONON
Bass, Vocals

TOPPER HEADON
Drums, Percussion

GUESTS:
Mickey Gallagher, Organ
The Irish Horns, Brass

Playing at pace and for greater stakes, The Clash had boldly evolved by the end of the *Give 'Em Enough Rope* tour cycle, but alas, Mick and Joe hadn't written a song in close to a year—a well-known hazard of the rock 'n' roll treadmill but also one that the guys would turn on its head, in the end proving more than capable of building a cathedral on shifting sand.

Shoving off their conceptualizing and combative manager Bernie Rhodes, The Clash in the process lost their practice space, Rehearsal Rehearsals in Camden Town, North London. A search carried out by tour manager Johnny Green and Topper's trusty drum tech, Barry "the Baker" Auguste, turned up a place close by in Pimlico called Vanilla Studios, a long and skinny room, a bit run down but private. There, beginning in May 1979, the band tested the waters by playing covers from across the rock spectrum and, importantly, well outside their clanging rock norm, letting loose their love of reggae, ska, and American music across genres. In the process, they almost forsook punk.

As the band has articulated, they had grown in leaps as musicians by this point. The playing had improved, yes, but they were also spurred on by the accelerated style shifts happening to punk; by lessons learned from Sandy and from their own longer songs, including a spate of creative non-LP singles; and by the burst of independence that resulted from firing Rhodes.

Touring the United States in 1979 after making the record, the band soaked up further inspiration from their provocative support choices, including the likes of Bo Diddley and the Undertones, as well as Sam & Dave, Screamin' Jay Hawkins, Strummer lookalike Joe Ely, ex–New York Dolls frontman David Johansen, lo-fi rockabilly outsiders The Cramps, and other local punks.

The band was also getting along great at this point, and they underscored their camaraderie by shutting out hangers-on as they wrote in their incubator, rehearsed to a strict schedule, fired neurons by playing regular afternoon games of football on a playground, and then fired them more by the boozing right after (which usually led to a second bout of rehearsals).

They would shock nobody with their strident, Springsteen-esque scoping of varied rock traditions because no one was let into the inner circle to shock. They would be more than ready when time came to record.

The Clash tracked down Guy Stevens at a pub and cajoled him into producing the record. Stevens had been an influential DJ, writer, producer, and label executive in the '60s and '70s, known for his vast knowledge of R & B, blues, and early rock. He had produced Alex Harvey, Free, Spooky Tooth, and Mott the Hoople, a favorite of Mick's. But his star had waned as his alcoholism and drugging grew, and the label was wary.

The sessions, commencing at Wessex Studios in August 1979, were perhaps not surprisingly raucous, with Stevens knocking over piles of chairs, throwing chairs, swinging a ladder, wrecking a piano by pouring wine on the keys, pouring beer into the studio's TV, and generally getting in the guys' faces while the quiet hero of the sessions, engineer Bill Price, picked up the pieces and dialed in the sounds of what would be a gorgeous sounding record. Stevens was so far gone he was quietly pushed out after the first two weeks of crazed antics and spotty attendance. Two years later, he'd be dead from an overdose of a drug he was taking to cure his alcoholism.

Despite the initial mayhem, *London Calling* would be knocked together in constantly inspired sessions over a five- to six-week period, with the band clocking eighteen-hour days toward the end. Paul, for his part, loved working with Stevens despite the madness, and everybody loved working with Topper, who spread his wings and utilized much of his jazz knowledge and training on the sessions, inspiring the band through the challenge of diverse styles to the point where takes were kept minimal.

Arguably there was not a single punk song on the resulting double record, but there was reggae, bluebeat, soul, New Orleans–style jazz, Phil Spector–like sounds, unabashed pop, dance, (polite) hard rock, '50s-inspired rock 'n' roll, and lyrically speaking truckloads of historical imagery, from the personal to the political to the cultural.

London Calling represented a shocking shift of artist identity comparable to Bob Dylan going electric or David Bowie going everywhere. But the gambit paid off richly and The Clash were applauded for a play of considerable courage. Writing in *Rolling Stone*, Tom Carson gave the record a glowing five-star review, stating "the record ranges across the whole of rock & roll's past for its sound, and digs deeply into rock legend, history, politics, and myth for its images and themes." The album would cough up three minor hits on its slow march to platinum status.

But more pertinently, *London Calling* was, and continues to be, lauded as one of the greatest albums of all time, consistently making top ten lists compiled by the most demanding of critics. With *London Calling*, there was no one left—outside of bitter old-school punks—who could deny The Clash the sobriquet of "the only band that matters."

LONDON CALLING

STRUMMER/JONES 3:19

The journey through the vast audio panorama of *London Calling* begins with the title track and, in fact, one of the weirder songs on the album. And weird can often be commercial, which is the case here, because "London Calling" has outlasted "Train in Vain" and "Lost in the Supermarket" from this record, and "Rock the Casbah" and "Should I Stay or Should I Go" from *Combat Rock* in representing the band's essence in one song—at least among any Clash songs that have been minor hits.

After seeing the track's production video featuring the band playing the song in the rain at night on the floating pier at Battersea Park—in the cold, too, for you can see their breaths—it's hard to disassociate that imagery from the song's novel and anxious up-tempo reggae thump. Nor would one want to—"London Calling" is a video for the ages, the perfect marriage of Joe's apocalyptic warnings (and seagull-like caws!) to gritty cinematography that suggests this might be the last concert on earth.

The track's title came from the BBC World Service station ID, which was most associated with World War II–era announcements broadcast in occupied countries. After making this grim historical reference in the opening lines, Joe quickly casts the net wider, referencing police brutality (drawing a parallel between swinging London and the swing of a truncheon), heroin use ("I saw you nodding out"), his February '78 bout of hepatitis ("yellowy eyes"), and the death of punk, referred to here as "phony Beatlemania," although, interestingly, the real *Beatlemania* musical had recently ended a successful run.

Acknowledging a generation's palpable yearning for something new, Joe also states, "Now don't look to us," reflecting the fact that The Clash were struggling, financially at least. Indeed, the band was deeply in debt, the last record hadn't taken off (stateside, anyway, though it hit No. 2 in the UK), and they were insistent that their new double album retail for not much more than the price of a single album, thus cutting profits for all involved.

But in his aggressive assertions that punk rock was a farce, that it had "bitten the dust," and that the band was not going to be held responsible for keeping it alive, Joe was also looking ahead with eyes open, grabbing the punk albatross by its neck and hurling it into the sea.

Which brings the song to its most apocalyptic and lasting lines, which address ecological disaster. Strummer references the recent nuclear

Despite initial mayhem, *London Calling* was knocked together over a five to six-week period, with the band clocking eighteen-hour days toward the end. Here the band commands the stage at London's Hammersmith Palais, June 16, 1980.

accident at Three Mile Island in Pennsylvania, the failure of world wheat crops at the time ("wheat is growin' thin"), and the OPEC oil embargo that resulted in gas shortages ("Engines stop running"). Poetically and enigmatically, Strummer warns of London drowning from an overflowing Thames, a coming ice age (much debated in the late '70s), and most memorably, the possibility of the Earth getting sucked into the sun.

The bed for these concepts is a thrum of a rhythm track, Paul gliding over the top of Topper's four on the floor, and his menacing first bass notes accented by toms. Oddly, Topper switches up his high-hat pattern mid-verse, from a triplet feel to a shuffle. He does this again for the second verse, and then for the outro verse he goes with quarter notes into triplets.

"London Calling" doesn't so much end as disintegrate, with Joe singing "I never felt so much a-like," breaking off before saying "singing the blues," a direct quote from a 1956 song by Guy Mitchell called "Singing the Blues" (Joe had been known to complete the line in live renditions). Morse code then spells out "S.O.S.," summarizing Strummer's assertions that the song was about everything slipping out of control, like The Clash creating a post-punk telling of William Butler Yeats's "The Second Coming" chaotically collaged from current headlines and turned into one of the most unlikely hits of 1980.

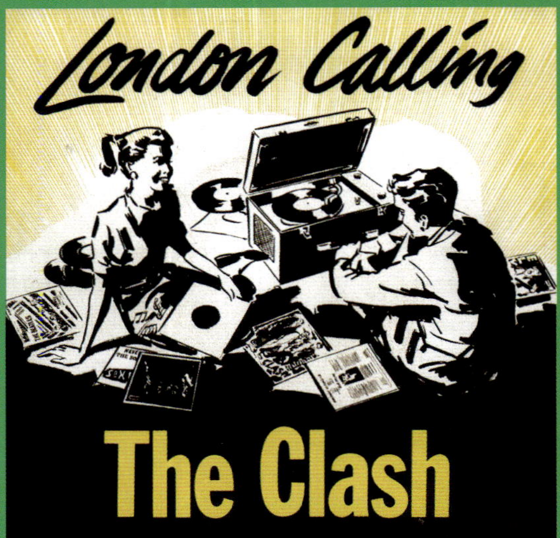

CBS 8087

CBS

Estereo

THE CLASH

LONDON CALLING 3:18
(Strummer / Jones)

ARMAGIDEON TIME 3:50
(Willi Williams)

Producido por Guy Stevens

TAMBIEN A LA VENTA

LP S 88478 (Album de dos discos)
THE CLASH / LONDON CALLING

LONDON CALLING

LONDON CALLING TO THE FARAWAY TOWNS
NOW THAT WAR IS DECLARED – AND BATTLE COME DOWN
LONDON CALLING TO THE UNDERWORLD
COME OUT OF THE CUPBOARD, ALL YOU BOYS AND GIRLS
LONDON CALLING, NOW DON'T LOOK TO US
ALL THAT PHONEY BEATLEMANIA HAS BITTEN THE DUST
LONDON CALLING, SEE WE AINT GOT NO SWING
'CEPT FOR THE RING OF THAT TRUNCHEON THING

THE ICE AGE IS COMING. THE SUN IS ZOOMING IN
ENGINES STOP RUNNING AND THE WHEAT IS GROWING THIN
A NUCLEAR ERROR, BUT I HAVE NO FEAR
LONDON IS DROWNING – AND I LIVE BY THE RIVER

LONDON CALLING TO THE IMITATION ZONE
FORGET IT BROTHER AN' GO IT ALONE
LONDON CALLING UPON THE ZOMBIES OF DEATH
QUIT HOLDING OUT – AND TAKE ANOTHER BREATH
LONDON CALLING – AND I DON'T WANNA SHOOT
BUT WHEN WE WERE TALKING – I SAW YOU NODDING OUT
LONDON CALLING, SEE WE AINT GOT NO HIGHS
EXCEPT FOR THAT ONE WITH THE YELLOWY EYES
THE ICE AGE...

LONDON CALLING, YEAH, I WAS THERE TOO
AN' YOU KNOW WHAT THEY SAID? WELL SOME OF IT WAS TRUE!
LONDON CALLING AT THE TOP OF THE DIAL
AFTER ALL THIS, WON'T YOU GIVE ME A SMILE?

THE POLICE WALKED IN FOR JIMMY JAZZ
I SAID, HE AINT HERE, BUT HE SURE WENT PAST
OH YOU'RE LOOKING FOR JIMMY JAZZ

SATTAMASSAGANA FOR JIMMY DREAD
CUT OFF HIS EARS AND CHOP OFF HIS HEAD
POLICE CAME LOOKING FOR JIMMY JAZZ

(E) 1980 Offset ALG, S.A. / San Raimundo, 31 / Madrid-20

THIS PAGE: "London Calling" b/w "Armagideon Time," UK (top left and middle right), UK promo (top right and middle left), and Spain rear sleeve (bottom left).

OPPOSITE: Backstage at the Civic Center, 16 Tons Tour of the USA, Santa Monica, California, March 3, 1980.

BRAND NEW CADILLAC

V. TAYLOR 2:58

Second song in, The Clash offer a cover of UK rockabilly Vince Taylor and His Playboys' "Brand New Cadillac," a 1959 Parlophone B-side. The choice represent *London Calling*'s second strong tie to early American rock 'n' roll, the first being, of course, the front sleeve's tribute to Elvis Presley's 1956 self-titled debut.

The significance of covering Vince Taylor lies in Joe's assertion that Taylor, with his rocker image, represented the start of rock 'n' roll in the United Kingdom, which got off to what locals sometimes classify as an embarrassingly late start due to the BBC, parochialism, and a focus on skiffle. Topper was more specific, calling "Brand New Cadillac" the first British rock 'n' roll song. Also a hit for various groups in Scandinavian countries in the 1960s, the song was later covered by Downliners Sect in the UK and was sampled briefly live by Mott the Hoople, which Mick, huge Mott fan, must have heard. In fact, Mick and Paul, living in their squat on Davis Road in Shepherd's Bush, had the record (perhaps the later Chiswick reissue) and were learning to play it even before they met Joe.

"Brand New Cadillac" was one of the many covers the band had been using to get the creative juices flowing leading into the new album, and it was not intended for use until producer Guy Stevens, in one of his first actions, taped the band's takes and picked one. Topper objected, saying they couldn't use that take because it sped up, to which Guy, huge rock historian that he was, replied that all great rock 'n' roll speeds up. (In all fairness to Stevens, if it does speed up at all, it's barely perceptible.) To be sure, it's a steaming, almost hard rock track, with Topper driving it, especially during the pounding last go verse before the band executes a deconstruction back to the *Batman*-like intro riff.

Lyrically there's not much to "Brand New Cadillac," but an interesting image is painted, in which a woman forsakes her man when another comes around who is wealthy enough to buy her a Cadillac. "Balls to you, Daddy" she says (this is Joe's addition—that never would have been approved language in the '50s), gleefully flaunting her new set of wheels, ignoring the pleas of the drape-jacketed suitor with Teddy Boy quiff on his head and brothel creepers on his feet.

OPPOSITE: Joe asserted that rockabilly artist Vince Taylor, seen here performing in 1961, represented the belated start of rock 'n' roll in England.

chiswick
BELINDA (LONDON) LTD
Recording first ublished 1959
S 2-A
An EMI recording originally released on the Parlophone label
BRAND NEW CADILLAC
(Taylor)
VINCE TAYLOR AND HIS PLAYBOYS

"Jimmy Jazz" finds the band in sort of an up-tempo pop jazz mode with a bit of Isley Brothers R & B thrown in. Civic Center, 16 Tons Tour of the USA, Santa Monica, California, March 3, 1980.

JIMMY JAZZ

STRUMMER/JONES 3:00

Of a piece with "The Right Profile" and "Wrong 'Em Boyo," "Jimmy Jazz" finds The Clash in a bit of an up-tempo pop jazz mode, with a little Isley Brothers rhythm and blues thrown in—bright and lively, like the happy bits of a New Orleans funeral march but with Topper's roiling swing underneath.

Playing along with Mick's cocktail guitar are the Irish Horns, a reduced version of Graham Parker associates The Rumour Brass, namely John Earle and Ray Bevis on saxophones and Dick Hanson on trumpet, comprising a classic New Orleans brass adjunct. Opening the song is Topper's drum tech Barry Auguste, a.k.a. the Baker, whistling over club sounds (Baker getting more involved with recording during the Vanilla sessions). The overall smoky-club vibe of the track, however, was the idea of engineer Bill Price, who took on more authority as Stevens became sidelined.

The intro sets the scene for the story to follow, in which the police arrive looking for the titular character. The drunken narrator either doesn't know where Jimmy is or does know but is evasive—in either case, he definitely wants nothing to do with the situation.

It's unclear whether the cops are threatening to "Cut off his ears and chop off his head" or whether that's a description of the crime they're looking to solve. Or perhaps the narrator knows that Jimmy Jazz has either suffered said fate or perhaps even had something to do with inflicting it on another.

While generally assumed to be a character based on a London underworld character, there has also been speculation as to whether Jimmy Jazz is a character based on Joe or on jazzy (in this instance, anyway) drummer Topper, or even if he's one in the same with the story's Jimmy Dread.

"Sattamassagana for Jimmy Dread" means, approximately (and cryptically), "give thanks for Jimmy Dread," as if Jimmy Dread has somehow taken care of Jimmy Jazz. The line "He sure went past," referring to Jimmy Jazz, sounds like a chuckle of an in-joke. (Incidentally, *Satta Massagana* is the name of a famed 1976 reggae album from the Abyssinians.)

Joe ends the song with a babbling, which, directed at the authorities killing his buzz, seems to say, "I'm too much of a drunken fool to give you any useful information on this sordid tale—leave me alone." It's a sensible fit to the song's ragged and at times jammy vibe, with Topper keeping things very casual and Mick turning in a bizarre and unraveled guitar solo with more fuzz than seems appropriate. By the close, everybody is stumbling through, dogpile-style, as if dead tired at last call or after a long shift.

16 Tons Tour of the USA, March 1 to April 27, 1980.

HATEFUL

STRUMMER/JONES 2:47

OPPOSITE: The line Mick sings about losing friends is widely believed to be a partial reference to Sid Vicious, who died February 2, 1979, three months before the writing of the song. 16 Tons Tour of the USA, Warfield Theater, San Francisco, March 2, 1980.

FOLLOWING PAGES LEFT: The Clash tacked a Paris show onto the end of their 16 Tons Tour of the UK. Three days later they were in San Francisco.

FOLLOWING PAGES RIGHT: 16 Tons Tour of Europe.

In the spirit of "Drug-Stabbing Time," "Hateful" juxtaposes a story of heavy drug use with jaunty music, the effect being the listener questions whether anybody involved wants to break free. The song's rhythmically twisted yet essentially 4/4 structure combines Bo Diddley (the band's main tour support in America in early '79) with melodic girl group melodrama. Shakers, handclaps, and bongos complete the production tour de force.

Despite Joe being mostly responsible for the song, the decision to have Mick sing it is significant in that before Topper's grave run with heroin, Jones was the one most on the edge; hence the denials ring all too true. A few lines especially clearly prove that the subject matter hit close to home. The dealer oscillates from someone who is a best friend to someone who not only charges for his wares but somehow manages to make the transaction hateful.

The line about losing some friends is widely believed to reference the death of Sid Vicious on February 2, 1979, three months before the writing of "Hateful" and the other *London Calling* songs at Vanilla Studios. But when Joe sings, "What friends? I dunno, I ain't even noticed," it reflects a coke or heroin user's dive into hateful self-centeredness.

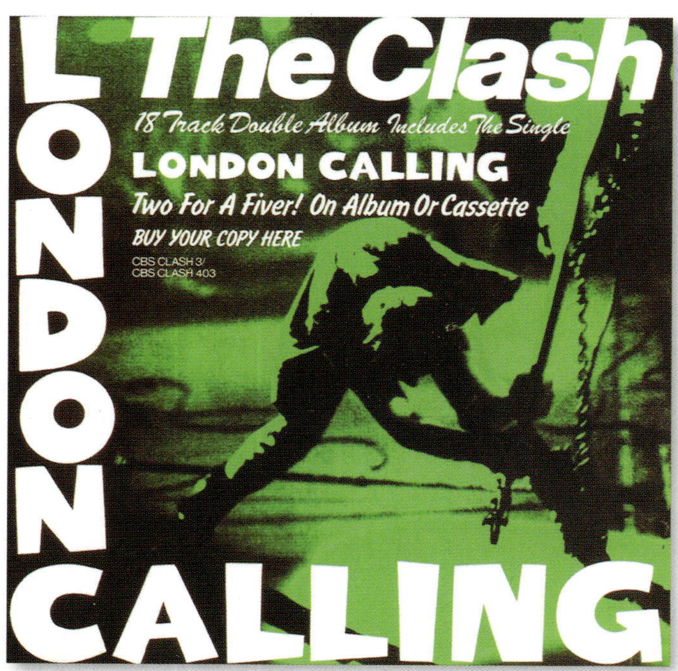

By this popping pop song's end, the narrator, almost detached from the situation, notices that he's killed all his nerves and lost all his memory, again, not too concerned about it, more just "grateful to be nowhere."

"Hateful" was played live just three times, all in July 1979 before the release of the record, at shows in London at the Notre Dame and the Rainbow.

THE CLASH
16 TONS TOUR
PARIS
PALAIS DE SPORTS
Mercredi 27 Février 1980

Present

TheClash

Live

Dienstag
13. Mai 1980
21.00 Uhr

VINTAGE ROCK POSTER Design by LUCA MALAGO

Metropol Berlin

Hornberger Waldfischbach

Rudie Can't Fail / Bankrobber
Rockers Galore..... UK Tour (Mikey Dread)
THE
CLASH
CBS 
CBS 8383
CB 111
Are Reg. Trademarks of CBS Inc. / Printed in Holland

RUDIE CAN'T FAIL

STRUMMER/JONES 3:26

"Rudie Can't Fail" can be considered The Clash's own sympathetic "My Generation" or "I'm Eighteen," told from the lens of a wide-eyed teen trembling at life's possibilities from the inside of rude boy culture. Ska music and ska fashion were about to explode in the UK due to the likes of Madness, The Beat, and the Bernie Rhodes–managed Specials (extensive Clash support in 1978) in their "cool and speckless" 2 Tone rude boy look, namely nice and tight "chicken skin" suits and porkpie hats of the sort referenced in the song's chaotic windup.

Musically, "Rudie Can't Fail" is a type of updated reggae, perhaps original ska, rocksteady, and reggae agitated by punk to arrive at The Clash's quite pioneering form of British-based modern ska. But there's also soul and gusto from salsa or New Orleans music. As with the song before it, "Hateful," there's a Bo Diddley feel in the strong rhythm of the guitars and rim-shot rhythm from Topper. Joe and Mick sing in duet, Joe opening by encouraging his bandmate with the evangelical "Sing, Michael, sing!" before the entrance of the Irish Horns and Paul's bobbing bass.

A few lines include specific references, for example "on the route of the 19 bus," which bisects locales where much of *London Calling* was written and recorded (the 19 bus, in fact, being Mick's ride of necessity). One gets a sense that Rudie is receiving bits of wisdom from his elders on the bus, advice that includes get a job, get to church, stop drinking brew (Carlsberg Special Brew—canned lager of choice in the Jamaican community) in the morning, stop getting into rows with whomever . . . mods, rockers, skins, casuals, metalheads, the police. Joe said that the bit about drinking Special Brew for breakfast referred to the band's own fond times in 1979 doing just that at "West Indian blues dances."

"Like the doctor who was born for a purpose" references Jamaican artist Dr. Alimantado and his 1977 hit song, "Born for a Purpose." Alimantado's biggest album, released in 1978, was *Best Dressed Chicken in Town*, which features a song called "Poison Flour," an issue-based "toast track" (toasting being a form of nearly spoken lyrical chanting) that inspired The Clash, among others, to be topical. Another inspiration was Desmond Dekker's "007 (Shanty Town)," with its refrain, "rude boys cannot fail."

The song's giddy music gives the track a sense of tenderness, the life advice being offered with sincerity rather than spite. The operative word here is "can't," with the rude boy feeling a sense of optimism that he won't fail, thanks to his developing survival skills and the kindly elder who similarly has decided he's not about to let the next generation fail without a fight.

OPPOSITE TOP: "Rudie Can't Fail" is The Clash's quite pioneering form of British-based modern ska with Joe and Mick singing in duet. 16 Tons Tour of the USA, the Palladium, New York, March 7, 1980.

OPPOSITE BOTTOM: "Rudie Can't Fail" b/w "Bankrobber" and "Rocker's Galore . . . UK Tour," Netherlands, 1980. The B-side tracks were produced by Mikey Dread, who also contributed lead vocals to "Rocker's Galore."

SPANISH BOMBS

STRUMMER/JONES 3:18

BELOW: Joe was enamored with all things Spanish, including the Spanish Civil War, partly because his ex-girlfriend Paloma "Palmolive" Romero, drummer for the Slits, was from Andalusia.

OPPOSITE: The 16 Tons Tour of Europe kicked off with a riot in Hamburg.

Breathtaking breadth of music aside, another reason *London Calling* had *Rolling Stone* calling it "the best album of the 1980s" is the similarly broad—and in the case of "Spanish Bombs," almost dizzyingly so—motion and energy to the lyrics.

"Spanish Bombs" references the Spanish Civil War of 1936 to 1939, in which Francisco Franco and the Nationalist fascists took power, fighting a coalition of the left-leaning Republicans and anarchists. Franco ruled Spain until his death in 1975, and at the time of the writing of *London Calling*, the ETA and the Basque separatist movement in that country was very much in the news. Strummer saw an opportunity to write about the current terrorist actions in Spain while drawing parallels to the sounds of Spanish bombs in the 1930s.

Clash roadie Johnny Green was knowledgeable about the Spanish Civil War and supplied Joe with reference material.

Joe was enamored with all things Spanish at the time as well, both through his inquisitiveness and because his recently ex-girlfriend Paloma "Palmolive" Romero, drummer for the Slits, was from Andalusia, which is namechecked in the song and was one of the first regions taken over by the fascists. Joe recalled actually being in a cab with his then-current girlfriend Gaby Salter when he turned to her and said, "There should be a song called 'Spanish Bombs.'" He was prompted by news of the bombing of tourist locales in Costa Brava, popular among Brits, designed to disrupt tourism to Spain.

The Spanish Civil War resonated with Joe as well because it was an ideological struggle between socialism, anarchism, and fascism, all three of which The Clash were already writing about passionately. This part of the struggle is colorized, so to speak, by the reference to "The Red Flag" a popular socialist anthem, and the black flag, black being the color of the anarchists but also many fascist groups through history.

The Spanish Civil War generated much impassioned art, writing, and protest literature, with poetry being an accepted and pervasive protest medium. Federico García Lorca, famed Spanish poet on the Republican side, was assassinated at the beginning of the rebellion in 1936. Referenced by name in the song, he is one of many martyrs among the artist class who died in the war. "Oh, please, leave the *ventana* open" quotes a line in Lorca's poem, "Farewell."

So many aspects of Joe's personality are wrapped up in the song. He continues to tie past to present with reference to DC-10s, the then-modern passenger jets that regularly carried tourists to Spain. In addition, DC-10s were involved in two tragic crashes in 1979. The ETA makes regular appearance in the song, too, but then Joe brings up the IRA, both being separatist movements, not geographically far from each other though vastly different in motivation.

Joe's ambitious time-traversing lyrics are set to a strident and lush musical track featuring surging acoustic guitar set against articulated slow-motion chords, plus vocals by both Mick and Joe, Strummer suppressing his punk shout and really singing, albeit in a key dangerously low for him. Strong melodies are generated both vocally, with the title-framing organizing device, and with guitars, the latter thanks to Mick's languid recurring lead line. Capping it off is some massaged-in Hammond work from Mickey Gallagher and a nifty vocal arrangement on the tricky Spanish bit, making for a Clash classic that's ambitious and substantive but also musically accessible.

THE RIGHT PROFILE

STRUMMER/JONES 4:00

Like "Rudie Can't Fail" and "Revolution Rock," "The Right Profile" would have to be held out of setlists due to its heavy reliance on horn lines as well as a sax solo. But on the album the song exhibits a kind of pop-accessible swing, with Mick adding familiar stock licks, its piano wandering around in the background, and Topper offering taut Mardi Gras single-stroke rolls against falling-apart fills.

And it must be said that, like those songs—and a half-dozen others, really—"The Right Profile" added to the shock among fans who thought they might get another dose of militant punk after *Give 'Em Enough Rope* and half the interim singles that were trickled forth. Really, The Clash are barely a *rock* band on much of *London Calling*.

"The Right Profile" relates the story of tragic film star Montgomery Clift, the suggestion coming from producer Guy Stevens, who handed Joe a copy of *Montgomery Clift: A Biography* by Patricia Bosworth, Stevens perhaps fancying something of himself in the notorious drinker and drugger. Strummer proceeded to read *two* biographies of Clift at the same time, amused by how much the stories differed and questioning which was "the right profile."

But the song's title actually derived, perhaps more cynically, from Clift having suffered a near fatal car crash on May 12, 1956, after apparently falling asleep at the wheel and hitting a telephone pole after leaving a dinner party at the home of Elizabeth Taylor, with whom he had been costarring in *Raintree County*. After his recovery, which required extensive facial surgeries to repair a broken jaw, broken nose, and facial lacerations, Clift had to film the rest of his scenes from a specific angle, or "the right profile." Clift died ten years later in what was deemed "the longest suicide in Hollywood history," following years of alcohol and drug abuse, in part to kill the pain from his lingering injuries.

Joe's limited lyrics begin with a roll call of a few of Clift's movies, followed by vignettes of him tearing it up in New York—and tearing up his face in the fateful accident. By the end, asking for Nembutal and alcohol, Joe becomes Clift and descends into his second bit of babble on the album after his police-fooling performance on "Jimmy Jazz."

Montgomery Clift, perhaps searching for the right profile.

LOST IN THE SUPERMARKET

STRUMMER/JONES 3:47

Never issued as a single, "Lost in the Supermarket" became an evergreen classic rock hit the people's way (i.e., through radio plays), with popular opinion over the years placing it up there with "London Calling" and "Train in Vain" among the handful of Clash songs allowed to live at classic rock radio.

The track's underdog status is all over the lyrics as well, with Joe inspired by the maze of lights and color and choice in a supermarket, drawing a poetic parallel to the feeling of disorientation and loneliness Mick must have felt being raised by his grandmother after being abandoned by both his mother and his father. Joe identified as well, having been sent off to boarding school by his busy diplomat father and nurse mother and left to fend in the harsh conformist environment—which he did, becoming a fast-talker; his brother, however, ended up committing suicide. Also notable, there was a regularly frequented supermarket underneath the World's End flats in Chelsea where Joe lived with Gaby.

As such there are two substantive parallel issues at play in the song. One is consumerism, searching for personality through shopping (guaranteed by the advertisers), and maybe even the human connection obtained by drumming up a conversation in the aisles. The other issue is the ironic loneliness of growing up in a flat of any sort but in this case a basement flat. One can hear the couple upstairs arguing, the pipes in the walls, the kids in the halls, people making phone calls. Comfort in both situations comes from one's modest record collection and emptying a bottle.

The soft and behaved guitar pop of "Lost in the Supermarket" becomes even more so with the application of Mick's wallflower of a voice, not to mention the defeat emanating from each heartbreaking line. Topper holds the song back as well, using a tom-tom in place of snare, an idea he had picked up after seeing Taj Mahal's drummer do the same at a gig the night before recording. Meanwhile, Paul wanders around his bass parts as through supermarket aisles, at one point running into a disco lick, which has the unfortunate effect of making the listener debate whether the song—along with "Train in Vain"—is in fact somewhat of a nod to disco. After all, it seems that by 1979, everybody was writing at least one disco song.

CLAMPDOWN

STRUMMER/JONES 3:50

First off, it must be said that "Clampdown"—birthed as "Working and Waiting" and often cited as "Working for the Clampdown"—is one of only a few hard-rocking tracks on the shockingly uptown *London Calling*. Whether there's much punk to it is up for debate, but this one, along with "Death or Glory," at least embodies some of that sweaty *Give 'Em Enough Rope* battle-readiness missing from much of the rest of the record. Sure, Mickey Gallagher plays a bit of organ here, but it's ill-placed and then, almost as if the band knew it, mixed far back. There's also a curious jumpy soul-into-disco part that nonetheless underscores the band's sophistication—this move certainly would not have been imagined for use on the previous albums.

Lyrically, Joe weaves a rich web of specifics and metaphor, giving the quite substantive and multidimensional word "clampdown" its due. The exact wording of the opening mumble from Joe seems to conjure images of the recently deposed Shah of Iran being whisked away, a substantial amount of treasure taken with him to make the rest of his life comfortable. Once into the main lyrics, there's a shocking, "Is this man a Jew?" (conjuring both Hitler and, closer to home, the National Front, given the turban reference) but then an artful shift into the main thrust of the song—the grind of the working man—through the image of "our blue-eyed men" being trained to be believers. Nazi youth or just kids fresh out of school and looking ahead to the immediacy of that paycheck down at the docks? Take your pick.

Joe and Paul have both spoken impassionedly and personally about one of The Clash's big early themes: the idea of escaping the grind of soul-crushing blue-collar drudgery, an idea most loudly articulated earlier on "Career Opportunities." Freedom, whether from a hippie's or anarchist's or punk's standpoint—is to be cherished, even more so when it's being attacked at the heart of "the best years of your life."

Throughout, echoes of the shock trooper opening remain, because Joe's line "You start wearing blue or brown" inevitably evokes various revolutionary uniforms

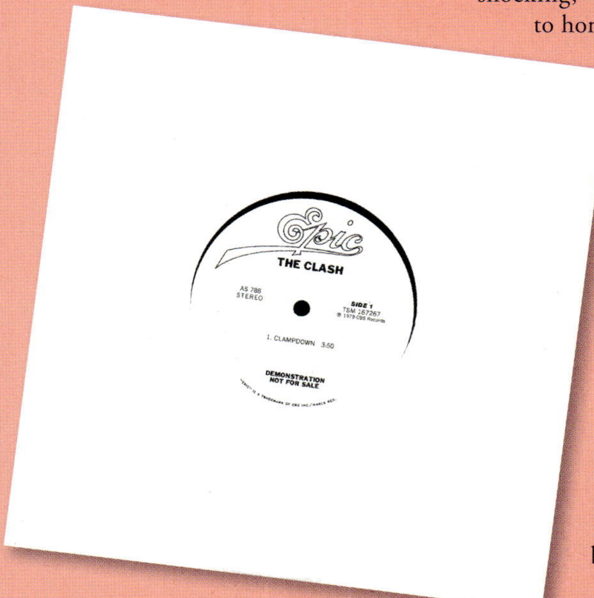

as well as Nazi brownshirts. Joe mentions *evil presidentes* and it all feels like a peek ahead to *Sandinista!*. In the end, things rarely turn out well for those whose spirits are squashed in the clampdown, whether they're under Soviet rule in St. Petersburg or cleaning up the nuclear mess in Harrisburg, Pennsylvania, where the worker begs to be melted down, suicide by capitalism. A hypnotizing death march of a musical outro—with chants of "work" from the blue-eyed voice of Mick—takes the listener out, accompanied by what sounds like the chiming of the Doomsday Clock.

ABOVE: On "Clampdown" Joe weaves a rich web of specifics and metaphor. Here he meets with William S. Burroughs in the legendary Beat writer's New York City apartment known as "The Bunker."

OPPOSITE: "Clampdown" 10-inch UK promo.

THE GUNS OF BRIXTON

SIMONON 3:07

Count on Paul to write a dub reggae for his first solo contribution to the band, a song about the significantly black south London neighbourhood of Brixton, where he grew up.

Paul wrote "The Guns of Brixton" very much to get in the songwriting game, although it didn't exactly open the floodgates. What's more, Joe insisted he sing it, which he does in a menacing monotone appropriate for a tale of gang violence, capturing the spirit of Brixton's ruthless Jamaican "yardie" gangs, which would be hit by the Brixton Uprising riot in April 1981.

Paul draws a connection directly to Jamaica with his reference to the iconic crime film *The Harder They Come* and its central character Ivanhoe "Ivan" Martin, who dies in a hail of police gunfire, reflected in the song's theme of police oppression. The character in Paul's lyric need not fear the "black Maria" (a police van), because he's going to get executed by the police, seemingly for no other reason than the possession of a firearm.

Paul says that the day he had to do his vocal, the studio got a visit from an American CBS rep, whom Paul glared at through the glass while he sang, resulting in an additional dose of punk snarl; live, his vocal pretty much abandoned any attempt at melody, descending into a shout. (Additionally, Paul, finding the bassline too tough to play while singing, would play guitar while Joe took over on bass.)

But Simonon makes his bassline count on the recorded track, which Mick counters with slashing reggae rhythms on two and four. Production ear candy includes a pile of intentional distortion at the open, lots of reverb and spookycore textures (including the sound of ripping Velcro) from Mick, and added percussion from Topper over his deft high-hat work and rocksteady beat.

The dub reggae of "Guns of Brixton" was Paul's first solo contribution to the band. In concert, he and Joe would swap guitar and bass because he found it difficult to sing along while playing the bassline. 16 Tons Tour of the USA, the Palladium, New York, March 7, 1980.

WRONG 'EM BOYO

C. ALPHANSO 3:10

Killing two birds with one stone, "Wrong 'Em Boyo" further connects The Clash to reggae specifically *and* to the vast history of American music generally. *London Calling*'s eleventh track is an up-tempo ska version of a song called "Wrong Emboyo" by Jamaican rocksteady act the Rulers from 1967 on the Rio label. The Clash here credit the song to Clive Alphanso (sometimes cited elsewhere as Alphonso), but the original record credits both the A-side and the B-side of the single to J. J. Johnson.

Linking the song to American folk and blues, the story related is the well-known and time-honored tale of Lee "Stagger Lee" Shelton, a flashy African-American pimp based in the riverboat town of St. Louis, Missouri. Christmas night, 1895, according to legend, Lee had been drinking in the Bill Curtis Saloon with crime associate Billy Lyons. A dispute ensued and Lyons took Lee's Stetson hat, whereupon Lee shot Lyons and walked out with the hat. Lyons subsequently died of his injuries. In the Rulers' version of the story, the two are playing dice and Lee catches Lyons cheating. Lyons then pulls a knife on Lee, who shoots him in self-defense. Variations of the song were recorded by numerous acts throughout the twentieth century, one notable example being the Grateful Dead.

The song begins as a strident and plush shuffle textured like New Orleans–style jazz but then breaks down, revealing itself as a false start. When it corrects—"Start all over again!"—we get a rousing pub-mad ska feel replete with defining horn lines (panned hard left), pumping piano in place of the standard reggae guitar rhythms, timbales from Topper, and a prominent Hammond organ (both panned hard to the right channel) from Mickey Gallagher. Gallagher helps turn the song into something we might hear from The Band, had they called Brixton home. With the song rarely played live due to the original's sumptuous production, Gallagher had to come on the road with the band to make a live version possible at all.

ABOVE: "Wrong 'Em Boyo" is a take on the American folk classic "Stagger Lee" (sometimes "Stack-A-Lee," "Stagolee," etc.) as heard interpreted by Jamaican rocksteady act the Rulers. Top: 16 Tons Tour of Europe, Hammersmith Palais, London, June 1980.

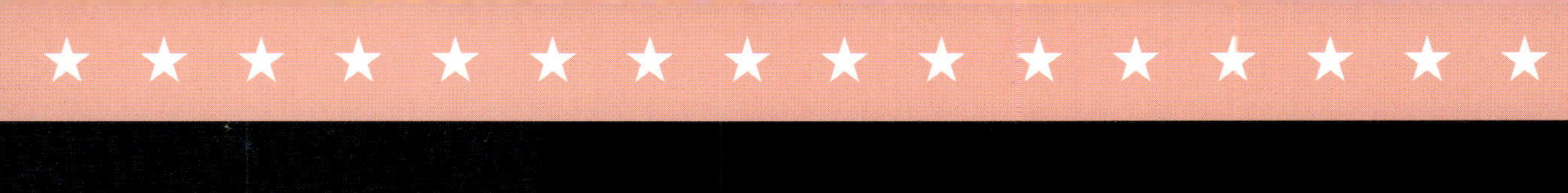

REPORTING FOR DUTY

MICKEY GALLAGHER ON WORKING WITH THE CLASH

As The Clash entered their prolific period, marked first by a double record and then the triple *Sandinista!*, the cast of characters involved would expand, with the band growing open-minded enough to welcome all sorts of collaborations. One of the additional musicians involved was Ian Dury and the Blockheads keyboardist Mickey Gallagher.

"The connection there was a company called Blackhill Management," Gallagher explained. "They managed Ian Dury when I was with Ian Dury and the Blockheads. And we had a PR guy called Kosmo Vinyl. When The Clash were making *London Calling*, they were scratching around, really, to try to get a really good album out. And Kosmo, who was sort of filling a PR function for them as well, put himself in the position of asking musicians to go do it. I was doing a Blockheads session at the time, and he just said, 'Oh, come along and play.' So I just went in one night to the studio and that was the beginning of the relationship. I had blue hair at the time, I seem to remember. We hit it off and we got on very well, but initially, I picked up a beer, and it happened to be Topper's beer, so there was a confrontation straightaway. First, 'Who are you?!' sort of thing. And Topper became one of the closest ones in the band to me later on. I ended up doing quite a bit with his solo album."

Gallagher continued: "Eventually I went out and did some gigs on the road with them, went to America with them. In my world, Ian Dury had just had a hit record with 'Hit Me with Your Rhythm Stick,' and he was recouping the rewards of that and he just decided to have a holiday for a year [laughs]. And of course, I'm a jobbing musician, so I was looking for something anyway. That came along and it proved to be fruitful on many levels."

OPPOSITE: Mickey Gallagher (background) onstage with The Clash at Hammersmith Palais, London, June 16, 1980, the first show of a two-night stand on the 16 Tons Tour of Europe.

Getting back to his contributions on the record, Gallagher stated, "It was mostly overdubbing. Because they'd laid down the tracks and they wanted to make it big, add horns, keyboards, and what have you. I played some piano but mostly Hammond C3. And I was probably the first one to overdub on the live stuff that they'd done. It was exciting to go up to the studio, and we became good friends. They were a crazy, crazy bunch and very interesting as musicians, in what they were trying to do. So the relationship just blossomed. My wife became good friends with Joe's now ex. It was all a very intimate relationship for years."

As for his impressions of the studio, Wessex, "Lovely, great vibe, fantastic," Gallagher recalled. "In a lovely part of London, leafy suburb of the north, just a really good vibe when you're in there . . . It was a big church, basically, so it still had the church dimensions in it. You had the big cavernous hallway where the congregation are, and the studio was built where you would have an altar [laughs]. The room was fantastic."

Another key addition to the team was producer Guy Stevens, with whom Mickey had worked in the '60s. "Mad, mad bloke," laughed Mickey. "I didn't actually work with him on *London Calling*, more so Bill Price, who was very good humored and easy to work with. Always a smile on his face when I was there and up for a laugh. But Guy was crazy, man. He was eccentric. A lot of these people who are eccentric, they have an amazing energy and creative power, and that was Guy. He used to create an atmosphere in the studio which was relentless. And manic. And that way, he put the artist on edge and got the work he liked from them. I don't know what it was, but he had a certain magic. It wasn't conventional at all [laughs]. Bill was more down to earth as an engineer. He was studio trained, so he knew the geography of the studio very well, and he had his own ideas of production, obviously.

"But the madness gets a bit too much when you're dealing with people like that," continued Gallagher. "It interferes. I wasn't there, but I do know the syndrome. When you're working with crazy people, you can only work for a certain time, and then it's going to go off, one way or another. It might not be anything to do with the creativity or the work. It's lifestyle. But he was also a music man, definitely, a music man, even though he came at it in a strange way. It was very drug-fueled at times too."

Mickey also arced back to the importance of Kosmo Vinyl in the melange of music that became *London Calling*: "Yes, well, first, he was sort of part manager. They were a bit directionless, and I think he took them and pointed them in the direction of Blackhill Management. Kosmo was the instigator of that, I think.

"He was a peripheral figure. He had a motormouth—he *was* a motormouth. At a time when the established record companies were losing power to the independents. There were lots of independent little record companies, right? They didn't have the money to throw into campaigns. They got a hold of somebody like Kosmo, who just came up with brilliant ideas that you couldn't ignore. And he was an in-your-face punk, and a well-dressed punk, very stylish, with his suits and stuff, dyed red hair, sort of a rocker, rock 'n' roll style. I think The Clash were a step out to try to expand his catalog."

Gallagher also figures that Kosmo helped shape the music that was to be on *London Calling* as well, however subtly. "It's sort of a seminal record, isn't it?" he asked. "It marked an era. It definitely gave punk a value. *Give 'Em Enough Rope*, I mean, it's very difficult to listen to, for me. It didn't have the quality that *London Calling* had. I think their ethos was, anything before *The Clash* is rubbish, yeah? Everything. It's a new beginning. But I think between *Give 'Em Enough Rope* and *London Calling*, they were actually influenced by Kosmo, you know, because he's a very knowledgeable and persuasive person. They would listen to it and absorb it and take it on. And you can tell that's coming through on *London Calling*. So it's a big turning point for them, and it turned out to be their biggest album as well."

Gallagher is proud to have been a part of *London Calling*—even if, as a rule, he was placed fairly far back in the mixes. "I just went in and did it," he said. "I didn't listen to the mixes afterward. I was just a conscript, yeah, very proud to have been on it, no matter how quiet it is. Especially then, they were putting themselves out as a guitar band. Because that's what they were, that's what they were recognized as. In fact, when I went on the road with them later, where they were starting to really try featuring keyboards a bit more, there were a lot of fans who didn't like it. And one of the first tours, I listened to the recording they did, and their own engineers had mixed me out of it. And I thought, what's the point? What's the point of being there, you know? But I never made an issue of it. Bollocks. But their creativity . . . that was the good thing about The Clash. They refused to be pinned down as any one thing in terms of their influences or how they approach a new album. I applaud them for that."

Gallagher (fourth from right) in his Ian Dury and the Blockheads days, June 1981. Mickey is between guitarist Wilko Johnson and Drury (in hat and shades).

DEATH OR GLORY

STRUMMER/JONES 3:55

One of *London Calling*'s very few hard rock tracks, "Death or Glory" is so heroic of chord structure that one can imagine it to be intended as a parody of the self-important past-their-due-date rock stars Joe spites in the lyrics.

Of course, vital and current and plugged in as he was, Strummer balanced his attack on '70s rockers (easy targets) with a more nuanced criticism of punks, thugs, and punk thugs—as well as anybody throughout all of time pompously proposing that what they've done in the name of art is of any lasting importance.

Strummer hits us with his best image first, what one can imagine as a wrinkly skinhead now faced with the grind of working-class domesticity, the classic LOVE and HATE tattoos inked on his knuckles. Joe has this old punk slapping his kids around with these same hands because they don't get it that their dreams also must die.

The cynicism in the song is made all the more toxic by the irony that Strummer has not only seen bands sell out all around him but that he surely must be seeing the strains of creak and rot in his own band in the form of the plush productions they were currently producing, through Jones's rock star tendencies, through the decline of Guy Stevens, and through the band's desperate financial straits at the time, which caused the guys to consider calling the album they were making *The Last Testament*, as in their last record and possibly the last rock record ever.

From a musical standpoint, "Death or Glory" surely swings for the fences, the band fighting the defeatism of the lyrics with the anthemic transcendence of Bruce Springsteen and Thin Lizzy and more so the latter this time, given the tasty guitar licks (including hints at twin leads), the low-slung and always dependable "Louie Louie" chording, the massaged-in acoustic guitars, and the deep rock pocket created by Topper and Paul, a skittering and ill-fitting break notwithstanding.

OPPOSITE: Mick backstage with producer Guy Stevens at the Royal College of Art, November 5, 1976. The cynicism expressed in "Death or Glory" surely was a partial reflection of Stevens' decline through the recording of *London Calling*.

X

KOKA KOLA

STRUMMER/JONES 2:05

It might be no more than a cheap joke writing a song about coke and Coke having the same name, but The Clash, as a band that matters, did a creative job of adding layers and nuance.

First, there's the historical fact of Coca-Cola originally having coca leaves (and kola nuts, which contain caffeine) as two of its key ingredients. Next, Joe weaves in some of the brand's catch phrases, namely "the pause that refreshes" and "adds life," while also referencing the big neon Coke sign in Times Square (the song is also partly inspired by the Epic records offices in Manhattan).

But the deeper message is how rapacious capitalists at the top cheat to compete. It's telling that the song was in part inspired by the band's visit to Epic Records' New York offices. Capitalism may work, but crony capitalism reveals rot, where its worker drones—even those running the show, for in Joe's eyes, they are drones too—need artificial stimulants to add life where there isn't any, in other words, not only to get the job done but to give what they do meaning.

Cocaine and (worried) party girls aren't enough for these guys, says Strummer. A vegetarian, Joe also decries their snakeskin suits and alligator boots, cracking wise to forget the launderette, they can take said garments to the vet.

The "play hard, work hard" system in the corridors of power catches up eventually. By the end of the song, Joe gets both ominous and smartly oblique. Coke is metaphorically a snub-nose .44, wrecking your health, but one also envisions a coke dealer showing up on the fifty-first floor, fed up with not getting paid and putting a bullet in his smug customer. *So freeze, man, freeze* means something different than it did earlier in the song, though it's still about survival.

Underneath all these great lines, "Koka Kola" (working title: "Koka Kola, Advertising & Cocaine") musically sounds very much like an advertising jingle from the '60s or '70s, propelled by the can-do steam engine chug of Paul's octave-jumping bassline, Mick's ethereal backing vocals, and Topper's jaunty snare work.

OPPOSITE: "Koka Kola," Joe's rant against rapacious, cheating capitalists was in part inspired by the band's visit to Epic Records' New York offices. 16 Tons Tour of Europe, June 1980.

BELOW: *New Musical Express*, December 15, 1979.

THE CARD CHEAT

STRUMMER/JONES 3:05

CBS got cheeky—if not meta—with this print ad for the release of *London Calling*.

Thin Lizzy must be mentioned here again, given Joe's and Phil Lynott's shared rapture with America, the American themes of the Wild West and gambling, and sweeping Van Morrison–esque music like "Death or Glory," "Running Back," or "Mexican Blood" to support a tall tale.

"The Card Cheat" sounds additionally expansive because Bill Price and Mick Jones (Guy Stevens had been effectively sidelined at this late stage in the production) double-tracked the entire song, including drums, to create a Phil Spector Wall of Sound out of it. The result is particularly plush due to the pumping grand piano and throbbing horns that are pervasive throughout, not to mention Mick's delicate yet impassioned delivery and Topper's light touch, similar here to that of Thin Lizzy's Brian Downey. And no guitars!

Lyrically, the song finds a gambler reflecting on his thrown-away life, before making the ultimate bad decision and putting down a king of spades he had tucked up his sleeve. This is not the place to be cheating, so it seems, because the gambler is now in the Belmont chair, i.e., a barber's chair, evoking images of the razor. The reference is also an in-joke about the old Belmont chairs Bernie secured for the band's rehearsal space from a stage and theater warehouse across the courtyard. There is also mention of a violin, the chosen instrument of death. The dealer tips off the clumsy ploy, and the gambler is summarily freed of a lifetime of regret (and drink and opium) by a bullet, as he pleads in vain on his knees for more time away from the darkest door.

Late amid the song's plush recline comes a clarion call to battle courtesy of the Irish Horns and an attentive military snare from Topper. The effect marks the height of elegance across the entire Clash catalog—if The Waterboys perfected "the big music," they got some help from "The Card Cheat." As the music takes a turn toward the historical, Mick laments the shared fate of soldiers across many wars who thought they could cheat death and win. We are told that wars are fought in the service of the king, thus recalling the earlier fateful king of spades. The final message is that however soon you think you are facing death, make sure to get in some love and life, for we know not when we will be tapped on the shoulder by the keeper of time.

LOVER'S ROCK

STRUMMER/JONES 4:01

Joe and Mick go full '60s girl group, which is not so much an anomaly musically (on an album full of anomalies), as much as it is vocally and lyrically. The title is a reference to a homegrown reggae subgenre becoming popular in England at the time.

Joe and Mick duet on vocals, Joe being Joe and Mick in falsetto. Lyrically, the song is a short, lighthearted, and almost adolescent look at the mechanics of sex and the magic of love (finding a place to kiss), in which certain considerations are alluded to: lovemaking skills, contraception (pill or early withdrawal—or a condom in case she forgets the pill), and abandoning the resulting offspring. Joe chides that "Western" man is too free with his seed. Later on, as he vamps, Joe references "You've Lost That Lovin' Feelin'," replacing "loving" with "grubby."

The music's playfulness is underscored by Topper's loose groove, Mick's meandering, Stonesy solo, and the song's slow unravel into a jam (albeit a disciplined and upbeat one at first) and finally a somewhat repetitive mess, with Paul losing the plot and all manner of vocal vamping and percussion novelty blowing it to bits by track's end. Topper's got his hands full with shakers and wood blocks before, amusingly, he switches up the beat mid-jam, reminiscent of "London Calling." In fact, he goes four on the floor, while Joe, almost as if noticing after a few bars, remarks, "Mostly on the floor now."

16 Tons Tour of Europe, June 1980.

FOUR HORSEMEN

STRUMMER/JONES 3:00

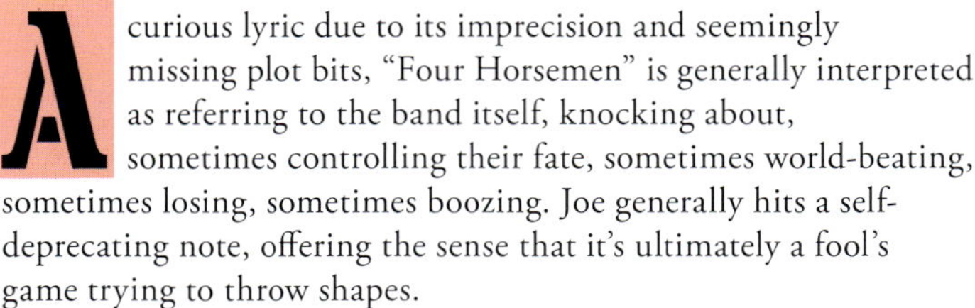

A curious lyric due to its imprecision and seemingly missing plot bits, "Four Horsemen" is generally interpreted as referring to the band itself, knocking about, sometimes controlling their fate, sometimes world-beating, sometimes losing, sometimes boozing. Joe generally hits a self-deprecating note, offering the sense that it's ultimately a fool's game trying to throw shapes.

The tone is matched by the up-tempo bash of the music, which is not so much punk but a generalized hard rock, something that might have fit on *Give 'Em Enough Rope* or *Who's Next* or *Who Are You*.

The song opens amusingly but speaking volumes, with a chord that recalls "A Hard Day's Night," after which Joe doles out his line about how wine "loosen(s) the screws at the back of the tongue," an image that suggests flattering by the record label gets bands signed on terms favorable to the suits in charge of the place. What ensues is a tacit agreement that the whole game is silly and that both parties will try to get one over on the other.

The Who come to mind again at the noisy mess of an end. Joe joins the jam, babbling about rock 'n' roll, prompting the identification of the four members of The Clash as the four horsemen, or, conversely, four rubes in the process of being trampled by the actual Four Horsemen of the Apocalypse, in the aggregate, fate.

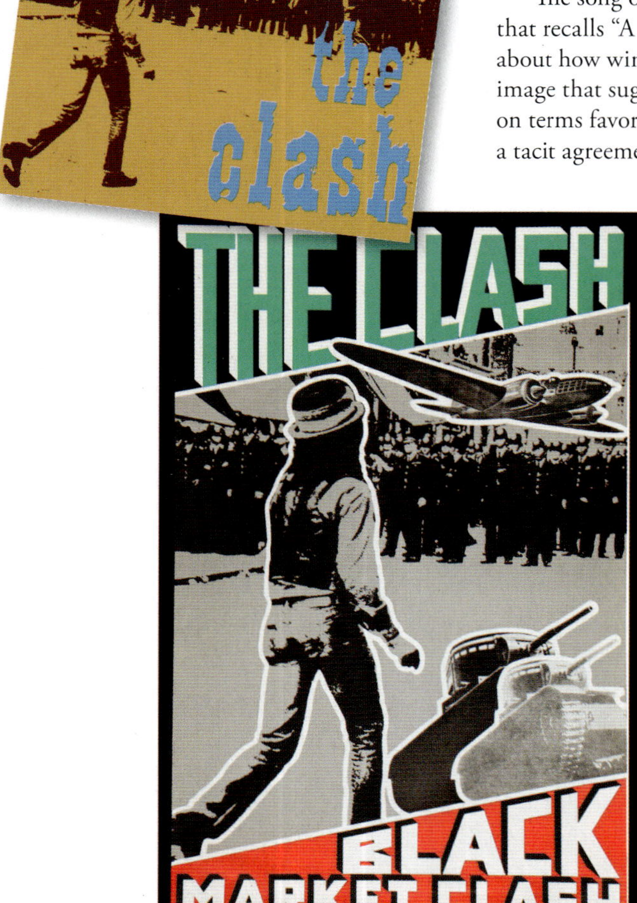

LEFT: Released in October 1980, the nine-track 10-inch EP *Black Market Clash* collected for the American and Canadian markets "rarities" previously unavailable outside the UK and Europe, including "Bankrobber," "Armagideon Time," the Booker T. & the M.G.'s classic, "Time Is Tight," and Toots and the Maytals' "Pressure Drop." The sleeve famously features a photo of Clash videographer (and later Big Audio Dynamite cofounder) Don Letts at the 1976 Notting Hill riots.

OPPOSITE: 16 Tons Tour of the USA, June 1980.

I'M NOT DOWN

STRUMMER/JONES 3:00

"I'm Not Down" feels of a suite with two other Mick-sung songs on *London Calling*, namely "Lost in the Supermarket" and "Train in Vain." Mick wrote the song while contemplating his own difficulties in the year leading up to recording the album—girl problems, money problems, drug problems, and, as referenced in the second verse, an incident in which he was set upon by a gang of rockers. Then, before Christmas of '78, with the band on the ropes and a next album not guaranteed, Jones had his flat burglarized. Shortly after, he split with Slits guitarist Viv Albertine.

In "I'm Not Down," Mick is reflective, speaking of how the rich aren't as happy as one might think, but being poor isn't much fun either. He also faces head-on the subject of depression, using a skyscraper as a metaphor. He's defiant in the face of all this adversity, an attitude reinforced by the compact and perky, almost jumpy pop of the band's musical track, later punctuated by timbales from Topper over a Caribbean beat that disappears as fast as it arrives. Adding to the sophistication of the track are two types of break and, to close, an interesting coda built of previously unheard jazzy chords overlaid with chiming post-punk textures.

"I'm Not Down" was in the band's set list for just three months. Performing the song for the first time, at Notre Dame Hall in July 1979, Joe acknowledged the sway the lyrics had over the music by asking the crowd whether anybody was contemplating suicide. Nonetheless, it's the chorus and its attendant sentiment that have lasted, the song becoming a *London Calling* fan favorite over the years.

OPPOSITE: 16 Tons Tour of Europe, Hammersmith Palais, London, June 16, 1980.

REVOLUTION ROCK

J. EDWARDS/D. RAY 5:50

ABOVE AND OPPOSITE: An early instrumental version of "Revolution Rock" can be heard over the closing credits of *Rude Boy*, a part fiction/part documentary film about a Clash roadie. The band disavowed the film when it was finally released in March 1980.

"Lovers Rock" feels like the cover on side four of the vinyl issue of *London Calling*, but "Revolution Rock" is in fact the nonoriginal. The third cover on the album and the second reggae cover, "Revolution Rock" was written by Danny Ray (with a co-credit to Jackie Edwards, due to a "Get Up" sample), originally appearing as a single under that title by Ray and as "Revolution Rock - Pt. 1" by Danny Ray & the Revolutioneers, both in 1976.

Due to the prominent presence of the Irish Horns, the album's sparkling cohesive production qualities, Joe's signature vocals, the political lyrics, the band's growing ease and affiliation with reggae, and the obscurity of the original, "Revolution Rock" fits seamlessly with the rest of *London Calling* while simultaneously foreshadowing *Sandinista!*, where it would have felt even more at home.

Musically, the song is layered with loads of percussion, from shakers to bongos and timbales, with the anchor beat featuring snare rim-shots. Mickey Gallagher is featured prominently and even gets a shout-out, with Strummer noting, "the organ play." The horns begin panned hard left, but then the panning is manipulated in a repeating pattern between channels, including a brief section of call and response between horns. Guitars occasionally respond to the horn parts as well, jabbing at them with an echo effect.

Joe sings the colorful and imagistic Jamaican lyrics with a bit of a reggae accent while throwing in a few words of his own, referencing the riot at the Rainbow in May 1977 with his "everybody smash up your seats" line, intimating that both reggae and punk are revolution rocks. By the end, Joe is vamping and ad-libbing, letting it be known that the El Clash Combo could be hired for "fifteen dollars a day, weddings, parties, anything."

The carnival nature of the track made "Revolution Rock" a live favorite clear through to 1981, despite the song's relative obscurity at the back end of the album and its status as a cover and very much a jam at that. An instrumental version from early in the Wessex sessions can be heard during the closing credits of *Rude Boy*, a lengthy patchwork of a film that is part fiction, part doc, part concert film—and fully disavowed by the band when it was finally issued in March 1980.

JACK HAZAN
DAVID MINGAY
DAVID MINGAY
RAY GANGE
JACK HAZAN
MICK JONES
JACK HAZAN
RAY GANGE
THE CLASH
JOE STRUMMER
MICK JONES
PAUL SIMONON
GAGA Communications Inc.
HEART & HEARTS
MELROSE
DOLBY STEREO
CLASH in RUDE BOY
ルード・ボーイ
メローなトンガリ、ストレート・クライ・シネマ。
ロンドンするクラッシュ

TRAIN IN VAIN

STRUMMER/JONES 3:09

BELOW: "Train in Vain" b/w "Bank Robber" and "Rocker's Galore . . . . . UK Tour," Netherlands, 1980.

Issued in the United States on February 12, 1980, as *London Calling*'s third single (backed with the title track), "Train in Vain" was The Clash's first Top 30 hit in the US, and it's not surprising the song did well, given its irresistible punk hook, nearly disco beat, and emotional vocal from Mick. The song's title is sometimes expanded to read: "Train in Vain (Stand by Me)," recognizing the repeated refrain. There was concern that calling the song simply "Stand by Me" would have caused confusion with the famed Ben E. King standard of that name.

The song was written one night near the end of the Wessex sessions and recorded the next day, to be used exclusively on a flexi-disc included with an upcoming edition of powerful English newspaper *New Musical Express*. But the deal fell through and the song was added to the album at the last minute, even after the manufacture of the album was underway. As a result, there is in no mention of it on the back cover, the center label, or the inner sleeve. The omission led to further confusion, with fans assuming the song was called "Stand by Me," given the preponderance of the phrase in the chorus and reinforced by the fact that the words "train in vain" are nowhere to be heard.

Neither do they seem to have anything to do with the lyrics heard. There are two proposed connections to the title, however. Mick has reflected that the song, with its pervasive and pumping harmonica line, sounds like a train chugging down the tracks. Indeed, if there's guitar, outside of the funk chicken-scratch at the beginning (reoccurring later), it's for all intents and purposes inaudible. What it sounds like is harmonica, piano, vocals, and occasional faint organ over a rhythm section (check out Topper's flams at the fade), although the live arrangement is one of no-nonsense guitarin'.

The other theory as to the title alludes to the fact that around the same time Mick had split with Slits guitarist Viv Albertine, who seems pretty clear that their relationship was the main inspiration for the song, noting how Mick used to take the train to see her in Shepherds Bush, where she wouldn't answer the door—hence, a train in vain. One further if more tenuous explanation that's been put forward regarding the title: some see the song as a response to the Slits' biggest song and first single, "Typical Girls," in which womankind is satirically discussed as every kind of flighty, fickle creature incapable of standing by her man.

ABOVE AND RIGHT: "Train in Vain (Stand by Me)" b/w "Bankrobber" and "Rocker's Galore . . . . . UK Tour," Australia, 1980.

16 Tons Tour of Europe, June 1980.

SANDINIST
THE CLAS

SIDE 1

THE MAGNIFICENT SEVEN
HITSVILLE U.K.
JUNCO PARTNER
IVAN MEETS G.I. JOE
THE LEADER
SOMETHING ABOUT ENGLAND

SIDE 2

REBEL WALTZ
LOOK HERE
THE CROOKED BEAT
SOMEBODY GOT MURDERED
ONE MORE TIME
ONE MORE DUB

SIDE 3

LIGHTNING STRIKES (NOT ONCE BUT TWICE)
UP IN HEAVEN (NOT ONLY HERE)
CORNER SOUL
LET'S GO CRAZY
IF MUSIC COULD TALK
THE SOUND OF THE SINNERS

SIDE 4

POLICE ON MY BACK
MIDNIGHT LOG
THE EQUALISER
THE CALL UP
WASHINGTON BULLETS
BROADWAY

SIDE 5

LOSE THIS SKIN
CHARLIE DON'T SURF
MENSFORTH HILL
JUNKIE SLIP
KINGSTON ADVICE
THE STREET PARADE

SIDE 6

VERSION CITY
LIVING IN FAME
SILICONE ON SAPPHIRE
VERSION PARDNER
CAREER OPPORTUNITIES
SHEPHERDS DELIGHT

Recorded at Pluto Studios, Manchester, UK; The Power Station, New York City; Electric Lady Studios, New York City; Channel One Studios, Kingston, Jamaica; Wessex Studios, London

Release Date
December 12, 1980 (UK: CBS FSLN 1 and US: Epic E3X 37037)

Produced by The Clash
Recorded and mixed by Bill Price
Engineered by Jerry Green, J. P. Nickolson, Bill Price, Lancelot "Maxie" McKenzie, and Mikey Dread (Version Mix)

RIAA Certification: Gold
Top *Billboard* Position: No. 24

SANDINISTA!

JOE STRUMMER
Vocals, Guitar

MICK JONES
Guitar, Vocals

PAUL SIMONON
Bass, Vocals

TOPPER HEADON
Drums, Vocals

GUESTS:
Mickey Gallagher, Tymon Dogg, Norman Watt-Roy, J. P. Nickolson, Ellen Foley, David Payne, Ray Gasconne, Band Sgt. Dave Yates, Den Hegerty, Luke 'n' Ben 'n' Marcia Gallagher, Gary 'n' Bill Barnacle, Jody Winscott, Ivan Julien, Noel Tempo Bailey, Anthony Nelson Steelie, Len Lewis, Gerald Baxter-Warman, Terry McQuade, Rudolf Adolphus Jordan, and Battersea

Pox on those who grumble the preposterous sacrilege that *London Calling* would have been better as a single album (one doesn't hear it often, but it has been said). Well, The Clash step right in it with the exhausting *Sandinista!*, for it's pretty clear that one could have shaved the triple record down to a double simply by eliminating the sound collages, jams, song ideas, near duplicates, and stoned studio wankery.

But this is all neither here nor there. Such parlor games, as satisfying as they are, don't negate the fact that The Clash delivered a full-on *triple* record, in equal parts to replay the broad explorations they got up to the last time out, to one-up Bruce Springsteen (who had responded to *London Calling* with *The River*), to give their fans more music for less money (although not exactly the price of a single album), to inflate their own sense of import, and finally, perhaps just to be perverse.

Sandinista! offers a dizzying variety of music over thirty-six tracks, all of which we'll get into, but let's just say for now that the album is a boundary-challenging follow-up to *London Calling*. There's also a sense of more dope being smoked, less discipline, less inspiration, and more reggae—and at the same time, an almost manic hunger for knowledge about the world and about the world's music.

No one would mistake Guy Stevens for a disciplinarian, but somehow, perhaps through the band's sense of desperation, *London Calling* emerged as one of those rare double albums that's faceted and refracting in all directions with intention and meaning. This time out there was no one in charge of the asylum and the inmates ran riot with the place—or various places, as *Sandinista!* was recorded in Manchester, Manhattan, Kingston, and back at Wessex in London, from where *London Calling* had emerged in its entirety.

Yes, producing was "The Clash," meaning Joe and Mick, with Bill Price doing much of the heavy lifting alongside increasingly knowledgeable and skilled Clash insider Jerry Green, mixing at Wessex, and other engineers at the various studios the band called home. Toaster and enabler of the "Bankrobber" single, Mikey Dread was essentially producer of the superfluous dub versions that cause the album to unravel on side six, bringing into high relief the missed opportunity to make a tidy double record that might possibly have been favored, depending on various imagined track lists, over the masterpiece that is *London Calling*.

Press conference at Bond International Casino off Times Square, New York City, May 27, 1981. In delivering a full-on *triple* record, were The Clash one-upping Springsteen, trying to give their fans more value, or just being perverse?

Adding to the sense of ramble mixed with disorientation is the fact that along with the gigantic swath of musical styles represented, *Sandinista!* features an army of guest stars, often playing instruments not typical of The Clash and even taking lead vocals. And so, frustratingly, one adds to the small pile of murky and aimless material songs that don't sound like Clash songs or songs that sound like novelty collaborations for release as UK singles around Christmas time or for charity events.

Production ear candy causes further vertigo, most notably on the dark side of the spoon and spliff that is the entire third record—with the end result being an album piled high with all manner of indulgence and yet mostly forgivable and charmed given the confidence among fans and critics that The Clash matter. Impressed by the gravity-defying musical creativity, impressed by Joe's action-stuffed lyrics, substantive and funny, people came away more than satisfied with *Sandinista!*, even if the more committed and thoughtful of them got there by playing God with the sequencing, comparing their twenty-four ideal tracks with those of their friends, delighting that the band offered too much rather than too little so that they could participate themselves.

THE MAGNIFICENT SEVEN

THE CLASH 5:31

First song, first side, The Clash let it be known that with *Sandinista!* they would challenge any preconceived notions of what constituted "Clash music." While "The Magnificent Seven" sat firmly on an R & B–influenced ska trajectory that began with four or five tracks on *London Calling*, it was made remarkable by Joe's odd and halting vocal delivery, which, alas, was no less than Strummer telegraphing the rise of hip-hop.

Strummer later said the inspiration for this intentioned early example of white rap came from visits Mick had made to record shops in Brooklyn, New York. There, he was turned on to the nascent hip-hop strains of Kurtis Blow and Grandmaster Flash & the Furious Five (the latter of whom had just released "Superrappin'"), as well as what is widely considered the first rap release of all time, "Rapper's Delight," issued in September 1979 and credited to an impromptu gathering quickly dubbed the Sugarhill Gang. While Blondie's "Rapture" gets much more credit as the first white rap directly inspired by the Bronx and Brooklyn pioneers, The Clash got there first, with "Rapture," albeit a much bigger hit, arriving the month after *Sandinista!*, in January 1981.

Another influence was the band's brief crossing of paths with Nile Rogers and Chic during their brief stay at The Power Station (previous to being kicked out when the money dried up).

It might be said that "The Magnificent Seven" represents the band's first experiment toward what The Clash would become across much of *Combat Rock* and *Cut the Crap*, not to mention the Big Audio Dynamite catalog of Mick and Don Letts. Indeed Mick, now sporting backward baseball cap, was so enamored with this new post-disco music, he gained the nickname Whack Attack and started carrying around a boombox transmitting the latest beats.

"The Magnificent Seven" b/w "The Magnificent Dance (Remix)," UK, April 24, 1981.

Although not electronic, the song is reverb- and beat-heavy, achieved by the band working with Ian Dury and the Blockheads bassist Norman Watt-Roy while Paul was away trying to make a movie. Watt-Roy, flown in along with his Blockheads bandmate Mickey Gallagher, was in fact responsible for getting the song off the ground, Gallagher instructing him to play something funky so they could jam while waiting for the band to show up for their first session of the trip. Watt-Roy would not be included in the credits, causing some consternation; others were not happy either about the simplified credit given mostly to "The Clash" across the sprawling and complicated collaborative album.

Working in March 1980 at Electric Lady in Greenwich Village (downstairs, with the Stones working upstairs on *Emotional Rescue*), Strummer breathlessly addressed one of his favorite themes: the grind of the working man and his susceptibility to commercialism and the machinery of the capitalist system. The press's inanity is addressed with "Vacuum cleaner sucks up budgie," which was a headline Joe espied in the *News of the World*.

The nagging ringing in the ear, so key to the song, evokes the start of classes but also an alarm clock, a fire alarm, Pavlov's dog, and the thrum and clang of New York City. Backing vocals drift in and out in a form of call and response, while Mick punctuates the proceedings with clean guitar stabs in synch with Topper's snare. Joe gets to make a bird sound on another record, replacing the seagulls of "London Calling" with that of the aforementioned budgie in distress.

Never issued as a single in the United States, the song has nonetheless been one of the few to live on from the record, its life extended through a remix version titled "The Magnificent Dance" issued as a single in the UK, as well as non-Clash remixes and plays on urban radio. No doubt its lasting memory also benefits from its placement at the front of an album comprising six sides and thirty-six tracks.

TOP RIGHT AND MIDDLE: "The Magnificent Seven" b/w "The Magnificent Dance," France, April 10, 1981.

BOTTOM RIGHT: "The Magnificent Seven" 12-inch, UK.

HITSVILLE U.K.

THE CLASH 4:22

OPPOSITE: To most ears Mick's American girlfriend Ellen Foley took lead vocals on "Hitsville U.K."

BELOW: "Hitsville U.K." b/w "Radio One," UK, January 16, 1981.

Only two songs in and The Clash are proposing themselves as somewhat of a collective. On bass, although little known at the time, was Blockheads' thumper Norman Watt-Roy, and on vocals was Mick's American girlfriend, Ellen Foley, purportedly dueting with Mick but to most ears taking the lead.

The song is in yet another newly explored style for the band, a type of pumping gospel girl group R&B nod to Motown as represented by the title, a play on Motown's Hitsville USA nickname. Sure, there's bass (again, not Paul) and drums (heavily treated), but the arrangement eschews guitars for harmonica, keyboards, and xylophone.

The idea of Hitsville USA is used only as a jumping-off point, the idea being that the UK, and not particularly just London, was having a fecund creative period, fueled by the seat-of-the-pants entrepreneurs running indie labels. Mick could have been talking about the punk scene or even the New Wave of British Heavy Metal, but he stayed current, namechecking Rough Trade, Small Wonder, and Fast Product out of Edinburgh, each figuring out at the time what to do with post-punk.

The song nicely captures the spirit of an indie rock 'n' roll scene, bringing up stolen guitars, the inability to manipulate the charts like the majors, no hope of sales over a thousand units, no testing with focus groups, no expense accounts, and "no slimy deals with smarmy eels." Rather, it's bang it out in 2:59 with a mic on a boom stand in some living room–turned-studio and release it to radio.

As they say in single-obsessed UK, "Hitsville U.K." barely troubled the charts, neither in the home country, where it was issued with Jamaican producer Mikey Dread's "Radio One" on the flip, nor in the United States, where the B-side was traditional Clash rocker (albeit cover), "Police on My Back." This came as a bit of a shock but was indicative of their punk base deserting them. The song, another of the band's non-punk production numbers, was never played live.

The
CLASH
DROP
THE
BIG
ONE

JUNCO PARTNER

JAMES BOOKER 4:52

The Clash place themselves in a long line of artists who would tackle this grimy blues standard, first made popular by James Waynes in 1951, with the song subtitled "(Worthless Man)" on the label. "Junco Partner" made the rounds over the ensuing years, covered by, among others, Aaron King & the Imperials, Louis Jordan, Michael Bloomfield, Dr. John, Professor Longhair, and Warren Zevon/R.E.M. supergroup Hindu Love Gods. Bob Dylan even took the title of his 1986 album, *Knocked Out Loaded*, from the song's lyrics.

Joe had worked it up as well with his pre-Clash pub band the 101ers, Strummer having taken a shine to the jaunty cajun–style version by Richard Hayes with its a cappella opening. Hayes's label, Mercury, deemed it "An Authentic Cajun Folk Song," subtitling it "(A Worthless Cajun)," and crediting it to Bob Shad and Robert Ellen. The original James Waynes version is essentially uncredited, but it had been recorded for Shad's label, thus Mercury's later credit to Shad and Ellen (a pseudonym Shad used). The Clash credit the song in error to James Booker, who covered the song on his album by that name in 1976, crediting the track to himself.

The Clash turned it into reggae and added production flourishes typical of their approach to the rest of *Sandinista!*—there's xylophones, horns, bells, keyboards, and violin, while Joe sings with an over-the-top Jamaican accent, which was in the spirit of the sessions. "Junco Partner" was recorded at Channel One in New Kingston, the band having booked into the Sheraton and quickly gotten down to work, recording with the Roots Radic horn section, their drummer Style Scott, and an elderly violinist associated with the studio. But it was the only track completed; thereafter the band was hurried out of the studio, making their escape in a tiny Renault because "the drug men" were on their way to either get paid or start killing people.

Lyrically the song is about a down-and-outer from the American South facing a sentence at the infamous Louisiana state penitentiary in Angola (indeed, the song is referred to as the national anthem of Angola prison). A junco (or junko) partner is basically slang for a drug buddy, and in the song, in order to keep the party happening, the wobbler in question dreams of raising livestock or growing tobacco. In reality, though, he has everything in hock at the pawnshop except his girl, who wisely wouldn't sign her name to the pawn slip.

No more inspired than the band's fresh and nascent reggae experiments on *London Calling*, "Junco Partner," with its quick-start conventional structure, represents the band as paragons of discipline, given the half-dozen or so stoned reggae collages sprawled across the expanse of *Sandinista!*.

OPPOSITE Advert announcing the incoming heft of the three-disc *Sandinista!*.

IVAN MEETS G.I. JOE

THE CLASH 3:05

"Ivan Meets G.I. Joe" features music fully penned by Topper, a talented multi-instrumentalist seen here with Paul in London in 1981.

Sometimes on *Sandinista!*, it's not just guest musicians but one of the four core band members themselves who gets shortchanged. With lyrics by Strummer, "Ivan Meets G.I. Joe" features music fully penned this time by Topper—he even sings the song, and quite capably at that—though it's credited to the full band. Of course the full band credit cuts both ways, as both Topper and Paul are conversely overrepresented by the full-band credit across the rest of the record.

What Topper, a talented multi-instrumentalist, wrote is something akin to a disco, or at least a post-R&B tune that is part disco and part early hip-hop. The main instruments on top of the busy rhythm section are piano and horns, again, like the last song.

Joe's lyric, perhaps inspired by Mick's quip that people would rather dance than make war, features an epic dance-off between Ivan, representing the USSR, and G.I. Joe, representing America. Dance-offs were a staple of early hip-hop, and the New York vibe is reinforced by a reference to Studio 54 (Le Palace in Paris is namechecked too).

The Cold War of choreography heats up precipitously, as Ivan proposes a nuclear attack and chemical warfare, with Joe responding by wiping the earth clean as a plate. Their various atrocities are framed as dance steps—appropriate, given that the longstanding East-West impasse was a dance of death. Shots fired are represented by video arcade game sounds, the aggregate chaos helping create the vibe of a noisy disco club. By song's end, the crowd gets bored—perhaps inured or desensitized—and subsequently shuffles along to see what China is doing.

THE LEADER

THE CLASH 1:42

"The Leader" demonstrates The Clash's ability to solidly outline a short story in a compressed period, this percolating rockabilly song being over and out in a scant 1:42. Part of this technique was the band's willingness to sacrifice choruses for verses but also to make every bit that remains contribute. To that end, the song is titled "The Leader" rather than words in the brief chorus comprising one line that suggests political sex scandals serve the additional purpose of selling newspapers: *The people must have something good to read on Sunday.*

Over a rollicking and echoey Eddie Cochran–like rockabilly riff, Joe relates fragments of what became known as the Profumo Affair, which aside from the alleged leak of government military secrets represented just another tale of British officials cavorting with call girls. The 1963 scandal resulted in the disgraced resignation of Minister for War John Profumo and the suicide by sleeping pills of enabling society doctor Stephen Ward.

The reference to a leather mask refers to the "Man in the Mask" swingers party discovered during the investigation, a titillating secret-society event at which guests were served by a gay film director dressed as a butler and wearing nothing but a mask, a Masonic apron, and a sign that read, "If my services don't please, whip me," hence the reference to a whip, with the added color being that it's a souvenir from the Boer War. Joe's inspiration for this passage was a newspaper article, a snippet of which was included as part of the artwork in the album's six-page lyric insert titled *Armagideon Times No. 3* (*Armagideon Times* being the name of the Clash tour program).

Like in "The Magnificent Seven," there's a sense that Joe is rushing to cram as much information as possible into "The Leader," but his method matches the hurried, energetic vibe of the music, the highlights being its rumbling train of a verse riff, the spare but thoughtful backing vocals, and the rockabilly licks dovetailed through the blink-and-you-miss-it chorus.

SOMETHING ABOUT ENGLAND

THE CLASH 3:42

Offering a superlative lyric that makes visceral hard times in the twentieth-century UK from the Great War on, The Clash end side one of *Sandinista!* with the album's first in a clutch of band classics.

"Something About England" begins with an homage to music hall, England's version of Vaudeville with roots dating back to the mid-1800s. Submerged and exhausted horns, played by military bandsman David Yates, session saxophonist Gary Barnacle (veteran of a few Clash songs already as well as a school chum of Topper's), and Gary's dad, Bill Barnacle, also a noted jazz musician, accompany a similarly weary Mick as he makes his way home late at night, musing about old England and how the upper classes imagine immigration has ruined what was once an ideal nation.

He then gets a lesson in hard times, from a dirty overcoat poetically propping up an old man, here played by The Clash's resident voice of hard times, Joe Strummer. The song becomes framed by the type of passionate pop melody Mick does so well, driven by a very grand piano and very little guitar. But the wistful and meandering horns remain—and remain faithful to the spirit of music hall—comprising one of the catalog's most sophisticated horn arrangements.

As the song plays out, Strummer's character drives home the point that old England was a lot tougher than rosy nostalgia would have Mick believe, with England thrown into depression by World War I, with starvation subsequently taking hold in the north leading to protests that marched south upon London. Mick's harsh historian further tells him of the psychological damage imparted by World War II along with the destruction of infrastructure through the German Blitz and then the threat of the "scientific sun," a reference, of course, to atomic weapons. A Pink Floyd–like appointment offers a mob of soldiers singing the World War I–era music hall standard "It's a Long Way to Tipperary" along with other assorted period effects.

The mournful conclusion is the reflection that, despite all the shocks to the nation's system, England's aggressive and repressive class structure remained, the implicit lesson being that those who suffered most were still disdained by those who "lifted cake to their mouths." And then the moon is up, the gangs having gone home. Lights turn off in spare and lonely bedsits, leaving old England—the authentic version just told, that is—all alone.

THE NEW 3 RECORD SET
or cassette
SANDINISTA!
★ THE CLASH ★
1
1. THE MAGNIFICENT SEVEN
2. HITSVILLE U.K.
3. JUNCO PARTNER
4. IVAN MEETS G.I. JOE
5. THE LEADER
6. SOMETHING ABOUT ENGLAND
2
1. REBEL WALTZ
2. LOOK HERE
3. THE CROOKED BEAT
4. SOMEBODY GOT MURDERED
5. ONE MORE TIME
6. ONE MORE DUB
3
1. LIGHTNING STRIKES (NOT ONCE BUT TWICE)
2. UP IN HEAVEN (NOT ONLY HERE)
3. CORNER SOUL
4. LETS GO CRAZY
5. IF MUSIC COULD TALK
6. THE SOUND OF THE SINNERS
4
1. POLICE ON MY BACK
2. MIDNIGHT LOG
3. THE EQUALISER
4. THE CALL UP
5. WASHINGTON BULLETS
6. BROADWAY
5
1. LOSE THIS SKIN
2. CHARLIE DON'T SURF
3. MENSFORTH HILL
4. JUNKIE SLIP
5. KINGSTON ADVICE
6. THE STREET PARADE
6
1. VERSION CITY
2. LIVING IN FAME
3. SILICONE ON SAPPHIRE
4. VERSION PARDNER
5. CAREER OPPORTUNITIES
6. SHEPHERDS DELIGHT
NO MORE THAN £5.99
CBS
FSLN 1

THE CLASH

REBEL WALTZ

THE CLASH 3:25

To evoke Pink Floyd again, sequence "Rebel Waltz" after "Something About England" and The Clash suddenly have on their hands their own dark chapter of *The Wall*, arguably saying more about the horrors of war with these two psychological head trips than Waters achieved over the expanse of the second best double album of 1979 or later with *The Final Cut*.

"Rebel Waltz" can be read as the reverie of a shocked soldier falling into a dream on a rural battlefield after the shelling has subsided, his dream state explaining metaphysical touches such as soldiers dancing on air. The war in which he's involved isn't specified, but the mention of rebels seem to suggest the Spanish Civil War, a subject dear to Joe's heart, though the mention of campfires and glades evokes an even earlier conflict: the American Civil War. There's also the evergreen war-story device of coping with the chaos and threat of imminent death by clinging to a budding romance back home, a rifle in this case substituting as a dance partner.

Musically, Mick picks clean guitar lines that almost sound like bass up the fretboard, while Topper methodically keeps a halting ¾ waltz time off in an echo chamber of his own lonely isolation. The music is disturbing and fitting of the fitful sleep evoked in Joe's lyric, which could easily be imagined as an event from the past World War II experiences of the broken-down character depicted in "Something About England."

The harpsichord, the psychedelic repeating horns, and the song's minimalism evoke a Stranglers vibe, but more to the point, what The Clash accomplish is to surprise us yet again with an entirely new musical style and arrangement, underscoring that *Sandinista!*, despite copious and unrepentant filler, contains a fair deal of music that represents a creative leap beyond the aggregate of *London Calling*, which is quickly sounding basic in comparison.

"Rebel Waltz" can be read as Joe writing from the viewpoint of a shocked soldier falling into a dream on a battlefield after the shelling has subsided. Backstage in Milan, Italy, on May 21, 1981, during the Impossible Mission Tour.

LOOK HERE

MOSE ALLISON 2:45

BELOW: On "Look Here," The Clash don't veer far from Mose Allison's original beatnik jazz idea.

BOTTOM: Impossible Mission Tour, Musikhalle, Hamburg, West Germany, May 12, 1981.

The best-known covers of jazz pianist and singer Mose Allison are "Young Man Blues" by The Who and "Parchman Farm" by any number of folks (Bukka White wrote it, but Mose Allison's arrangement became the most celebrated), including Cactus and Blue Cheer. The Clash threw their name in the circle and proved they understood the charms of this this prolific beat favorite, who died in November 2016 from natural causes at the ripe old age of eighty-nine.

"Look Here," in its original 1964 form, is pretty much a beatnik jazz tune, and The Clash don't veer far from that idea, lending it a bit more zip and 4/4 drive, the key performance coming from Topper, who championed covering the tune. But along with the snap of Topper's skillful snare and high-hat interplay comes a rock-solid walking bassline, piano, occasional blues harmonica, marimba, and Mick's mixed back licks and multitracked vocal, on which he convincingly plays the part of a '50s hipster admonishing a pal living his life too fast.

More than anything, the song contributes to the idea of *Sandinista!* as a work straddling the history of modern music, transcending conventional bass/guitar/drums instrumentation and, in this case, presenting a faithful jazz cover that is essentially a thousand miles from punk in every department.

THE CROOKED BEAT

THE CLASH 5:28

Paul returns to his London neighborhood and the dense influence of reggae found therein for a second time, following up *London Calling*'s "The Guns of Brixton" by penning "The Crooked Beat." As with the former, Simonon's vocal delivery is laconic, monotone even, the voice of a working-class ruffian staking territory.

Also as with the former, "The Crooked Beat" ends in police harassment of the locals. Here, those reducing tension with the crooked beat—the cymbal splash, the rocking bass and drum—get hauled off to jail, *one and all*. This final turn of events plays out to a verse reminiscent of the children's rhyme "There Was a Crooked Man."

"The Crooked Beat" was never played live, perhaps because Paul already had a showcase song but also possibly because of its use of horns, organ, and piled-up echo and reverb effects, not to mention the fluttery rim shot and flam rhythm worked up by Topper and appearance of Mikey Dread amid much stoned studio gimmickry.

Nor was the song particularly "written," falling somewhat at the uninspired end of the album's compositions in terms of ambition and arrangement. No surprise, really, given that the band was back at Wessex and just looking to fill up the triple album to which they'd committed themselves. In fact, at the halfway point, the song collapses into a dub version of itself, dramatically underscoring the idea that The Clash intended simply to jam out the rest of the material needed to bloat the album past the missed opportunity to make it a fantastic double.

mpossible Mission Tour, Musikhalle, Hamburg, West Germany, May 12, 1981.

LE PALACE
présente
au THEATRE MOGADOR
25 rue Mogador 75009
Vendredi 25 Septembre 1981
CLASH
special guest · THE BEAT
50 frs
à 18 H 30
VINTAGE ROCK POSTER Design by LUCA MALAGO

SOMEBODY GOT MURDERED

THE CLASH 3:42

The seed for "Somebody Got Murdered" came from famed producer Jack Nitzsche, who had asked Joe to come up with a "heavy" rock tune for use in the William Friedkin film *Cruising*, starring Al Pacino. (Nitzsche, known for his work with Phil Spector, the Rolling Stones, and Neil Young, also pressed notoriously unprolific first-wave L.A. punk band the Germs to write for the soundtrack.) Joe later stated that the band sent the song off to Nitzsche and never heard from him again. Who knows whether it wasn't heavy enough, but it is possible it was too much of a scene-stealer, being one of the gems across the six sides of *Sandinista!*, a fan favorite, and a live staple right up until Mick's last gig with the band, the US Festival, where it was played valiantly but out of tune.

Joe's inspiration for the lyric came from the fact that after speaking with Nitzsche on the phone, he returned home to the flat he shared with girlfriend Gaby Salter in the World's End housing estate to find the parking attendant lying dead in a pool of blood just outside the parking booth, murdered over five pounds. Joe wrote the lyrics that night and gave them to Mick, who wrote the music.

Joe refers to the scene near his flat but also addresses the impact of murder on those around, in the first verse painting the picture of a gang of guilty parties drinking off the memory. Joe also ponders the finality of the act, along with the level of desperation that would lead to such a crime. Turning back to the specific event, Joe laments that once the blood is cleaned up, the crowd will disperse and little more will be said.

"Somebody Got Murdered" is one of arguably four to five up-tempo guitar-charged tracks on the entire *Sandinista!* album (unused was a short, spirited pop rocker called "Blonde Rock and Roll"), and it's possibly the finest, featuring inspired and heroic *Give 'Em Enough Rope*–worthy melodies from Mick to go with his intense yet feather-light vocal and his guitar phrasings. Other appointments include a recurring synthesizer lick that sounds like a spring unwinding, along with a dog barking, specifically Topper's very protective dog, Battersea, whose performance was prompted by Joe "thumping" his master.

OPPOSITE: Poster from eight-night Paris residency in support of *Sandinista!*.

ONE MORE TIME

THE CLASH 3:32

OPPOSITE: With "One More Time" the band managed a reggae with lyrical references to the American Civil Rights movement, poverty, and—kung fu.

BELOW: A period promo poster traces the many and varied influences on *Sandinista!*

A collaboration between the band and Mikey Dread, who toasts and duets with Joe on the meandering track, is arguably the clunkiest reggae on the album, outside of the dubs, albeit admittedly a live fan favorite. The song heaves and wheezes atop a four-on-the-floor beat, further hobbled by ill-advised production choices, including the drum sound, reverb-drenched guitar, murky piano, and a listless, unmelodic vocal. Like "Radio Clash," this one tries the patience, with its dour chorus of "one more time if you please," which is uncharacteristically awkward, as well as pointless, when considered in the canon of Strummer phraseology.

Lyrically, references to Montgomery, Alabama, and the Watts riots in L.A. place the song unmistakably in America. Other flashpoints include a reference to silicone, although it's believed Joe meant silicon, as in computer chips, given that he makes a point about "calculating" poverty.

As well, one can't help but think that it's New York City Strummer is thinking about when he talks about an old lady who knows karate and a baby who does kung fu. Joe had been soaking up New York hip-hop culture prior to the making of *Sandinista!*, and karate moves had infiltrated the nascent dance moves of the scene, inevitable after the half-dozen years of kung fu mania that had erupted all over America after Bruce Lee's fourth film, *Enter the Dragon*, in 1973. The movie also included in its cast black martial artist Jim Kelly, further boosting the movie's popularity in hip-hop culture.

Also driving the kung fu craze was the fact that Bruce Lee died mysteriously just as *Dragon* was being issued, either from a brain aneurism or a reaction to a painkiller given for reasons unknown. Topper was a professed Bruce Lee nut, as evidenced by the yellow jumpsuit he wore just like Lee's, beginning in 1978.

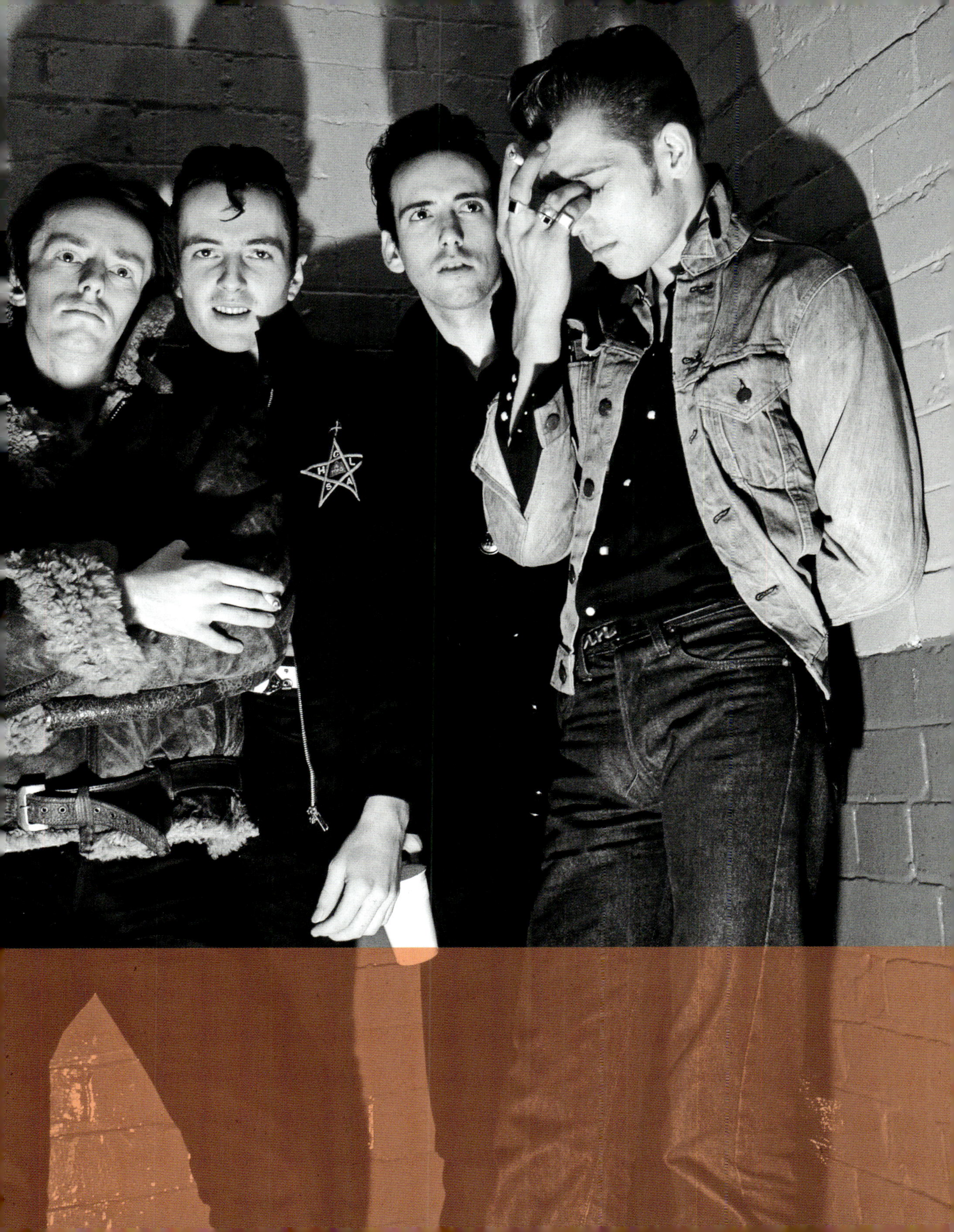

ONE MORE DUB

THE CLASH 3:34

The only named dub version on *Sandinista!* is dominated by Mikey Dread's grating use of a flanger on Topper's high-hat, with the underlying track being a standard dub deconstruction of "One More Time," with only occasional fragments of Joe's vocal and a couple of spots featuring Mikey, at the beginning saying, "Stop wasting time" (if only!) and then fading at the close.

Some nice suspensions of the beat and manipulations of the bass drum add at least a modicum of tension or plot; indeed, a careful listen reveals much for budding engineers to discuss.

With America still getting used to the non-punk Clash of *London Calling*, some might consider it quite brave—or perhaps even daft—of The Clash to push so much straight-up reggae, let alone the meta reggae of the album's dub tracks. Then again, one thing that made The Clash great was their fervent belief in following their own personal tastes, even if they led to seemingly ill-advised conclusions that only true artists would dare embrace.

Mikey Dread performs with The Clash in New York City, March 7, 1980. With "One More Dub," Dread and The Clash left much for budding engineers to discuss.

LIGHTNING STRIKES (NOT ONCE BUT TWICE)

THE CLASH 4:49

So much of *Sandinista!* was inspired by New York City musically and lyrically, but listening to “Lightning Strikes (Not Once but Twice)” is like perching at the top of a double-decker tour bus and letting the driver deal with Manhattan traffic, even if in the song, Joe suggests peeling off a pile of cash and taking a tour by taxi.

Of course, this was a rougher Manhattan than today—Joe points out Harlem slums, graffiti, pot that’s cheaper than booze, and one lone tree in Garbage Park. Still, the vibe is upbeat, referencing the many cultures (Chinese, Cuban, Jewish, Puerto Rican, and now British) making the city hum and thrum.

Interestingly, Joe recycles the vocal melody and proto-rap patter of “The Magnificent Seven” while Topper’s beat recalls his work on that song as well (as does the use of opening bells). But the overall effect is entirely different—funkier, with less of a reggae or ska link, and rather slanted and enchanted with jazzy piano throughout. Alas, it’s also even more repetitive and wordy, with a faint and muddy violin part that is pure irritation. If the band was hoping for lightning to strike twice, it didn’t happen. Neither “Lightning Strikes” nor “The Magnificent Seven” became much of a hit or a fan favorite.

“Lightning Strikes (Not Once but Twice),” in which Joe suggests lighting out for a tour of the Big Apple by taxi.

FSLN
UN PUEBLO
EN LUCHA

UP IN HEAVEN (NOT ONLY HERE)

THE CLASH 4:32

Waving away the blue smoke of the spliff bunker (a writing hovel built out of flight cases at Electric Lady and at Wessex), Mick and Joe muster some discipline, writing tightly and taking us back to the "reality estates," namely the "crumbling blocks" of working-class flats around London, where dead-end kids piss in the elevators, marriages are doomed from the start, and the youth still tag the walls with graffiti.

Musically, Mick cooks up mournful yet melodic post-punk pop akin to The Cure, Boomtown Rats, or early U2, his vocal style perfect for the tale's sense of powerlessness in the face of injustice. Distinguishing the song from so much nonsense on *Sandinista!*, the verse enters amusingly quickly, with Topper toggling two variations of his 4/4 beat verse to verse, grooving joyously with the responding bass part. Mick's chords are dramatic and punctuating, and his guitar chimey and textured, in dialog with Mickey Gallagher's prominent pub-rocking organ. The result is one of the record's classics, very much an anthem that would have been worthy of inclusion on *London Calling*.

The song evokes the story of the Ronan Point tower collapse of 1968, in which a gas leak caused the corner of a twenty-two-story block of flats in East London to collapse, killing four. It was later determined that construction standards were such that similar buildings couldn't withstand much in the way of minor gas explosions, fires, or even wind (a happenstance that is referenced in the song). Several books were written on the disaster and it was extensively covered on TV, resulting in an uproar and, ultimately, more stringent building codes. Even so, the horrific Grenfell Tower fire of June 14, 2017, demonstrates that there is much work still to be done.

"Up in Heaven (Not Only Here)" ends with an extended quote from protest folkie Phil Ochs and his song "United Fruit," which documents the various worker exploitation abuses in the fruit industry. Joe cherry-picks the lines that relate directly to the UK experience, intimating that the shoddy housing is created by the very system enslaving the workers so that they can scramble home and recharge to the minimum strength levels required to punch the clock the next day, which perhaps is sarcastically indicated by the deceptively happy jamming of the false ending.

Still, the overriding sentiment to take away from the song, as with "Lost in the Supermarket," is that Joe is writing with great empathy about his perceptions of Mick's past, specifically his life in Wilmcote House and the obstacles he overcame growing up.

OPPOSITE: London, 1981. On "Up in Heaven" Mick cooked up mournful/melodic post-punk pop akin to The Cure, Boomtown Rats, or early U2.

CORNER SOUL

THE CLASH 2:42

OPPOSITE: Despite the simmering violence alluded to in Joe's lyric, "Corner Soul" is effortlessly enjoyable from a musical perspective. Backstage in London, 1981.

"Corner Soul" further demonstrates The Clash's ability to develop reggae/pop hybrids that promote the view that the music that is at the core of *Sandinista!* has links to myriad Latin and Caribbean traditions. If elsewhere we get rigid 4/4 reggae, celebratory reggae, dark reggae, reggae mixed with calypso, and reggae mixed with modern funk and dub, here we are treated to a lush and melodic embrace of a type of soul music leaning toward a style characteristically explored by the roots reggae acts of the late 1970s, such as Steel Pulse, Black Uhuru, Burning Spear, Peter Tosh, the Gladiators, and Max Romeo, whose "War ina Babylon" is said to be a direct influence on "Corner Soul."

Using imagery of groves, machetes, beating drums, oil, diesel, and other trappings of Latin American conflict, Joe's lyrics address growing unrest in English neighborhoods such as St. Pauls (Bristol), Toxteth (Liverpool), Moss Side (Manchester), and Brixton (London), all of which experienced riots either in 1980 or 1981 due to high unemployment and racial tensions. Of course, the Notting Hill riot was addressed on the first record, both in song and on the back cover art.

Joe questions whether this music the band had embraced over a shockingly short period of time could be calling for "rivers of blood." It was a direct reference to conservative British politician Enoch Powell, whose 1968 anti-immigration speech represented a shocking level of racism at the highest levels of government, which in turn found enough support from the general public to cause deep divisions. Whether the conflict is exacerbated by reggae, the implication is that war has been declared, with Strummer trying to make the point that it doesn't have to be. In light of the rioting that was to come, lasting deep into the '80s, the song seems remarkably prescient.

Despite the simmering violence of the words, musical elements make the track effortlessly enjoyable—and even joyous. These range from Topper's novel snare beat to the pervasive sublime harmonica to Joe's intensely empathetic delivery to gorgeous backup vocals from Ellen Foley, whose rich and husky voice adds personality to parts that could have been mere window-dressing but which, in her hands, help the track to bloom and beam.

FSLN

LET'S GO CRAZY

THE CLASH 4:24

Impossible Mission Tour, Eissporthall, West Berlin, May 18, 1981.

Very much like "Corner Soul," "Let's Go Crazy" addresses a black uprising, but where the song sequenced just before it couches the struggle in Latin American imagery, this track is rife with reggae and Rasta imagery, yet not set to any sort of reggae but rather percussion-rich steel-band Caribbean Soca, as The Clash continue to explore all manner of world music.

Offering less of an ominous warning of what's to come than does its preceding track, "Let's Go Crazy" is a celebration of progress, with the drumming away of four hundred years of dread representing an end to colonialism and slavery. The reference to the White Star liner sinking at the dock signified a similar severing of ties between England and Jamaica, White Star being the English shipping company that carried trade goods and people between the UK and its former colony. There's also reference to calypso king Mighty Sparrow, and dreads are jerking their locks, pans are being played—it's time to go crazy.

But then the modern forces of oppression in Britain conspire to put an end to the smoking and drinking and shut down the party. Arrests and rioting ensue. Given the ecstatic soundtrack, it all seems playful, par for the course, accepted, almost like an agreement between the neighborhood and the police that this will play out and nobody will get hurt. Indeed, the party seems to be in full swing as the song closes hot, with mentions of "that sledgehammer sound," jamdown town (Jamaica), moa ambassa (the conquering lion of the tribe of Judah, Ethiopean Emperor Haile Selassie I, hailed by Rastafarians as the returned messiah), and importantly, Carnival. Note that violence and Carnival come together in the Notting Hill riot that inspired "White Riot" and that the song features reggae artist Ansil Collins making a plea for peace at Carnival time.

It's quite impressive how recurring and specific themes throughout the record link Jamaica and Latin America to the working class of the UK, and in widening gyres, to many facets of the band's New York experience. If *Sandinista!* largely unwinds and underachieves musically, lyrically, it is focused and substantive, becoming complex of concept and in this regard at least, befitting the expanse of a triple record.

IF MUSIC COULD TALK

THE CLASH/DREAD 4:36

The Clash craft yet another song that's not a reggae but that comes with a reggae vibe. "If Music Could Talk" sounds like the type of mellow New York soul Lou Reed would write. It's a jam, with bass and drums creating a loping reggae backline, accompanied by muted rhythm guitar and spare jazzy piano. Dominating the proceedings from a musical standpoint is session sax player Gary Barnacle, who solos throughout. And then there's Joe, who adds a dreamy pair of ad-libs, one in the left channel, one in the right, in this manner offering two parallel lyrics.

Recorded at Wessex in London, the song is essentially a more accessible version of "Shepherds Delight" (see page 179), which was also recorded with Mikey Dread, who got a writing credit on both. For obvious reasons (that is, because it features two Joe Strummers and is otherwise essentially a sax solo), the song was never performed live, although Joe sometimes said it was his favorite Clash song of all time.

Lyrically, Joe re-creates an inner dialogue with himself, reflecting on what it means to make music with his band, thinking about the people and the cultures that make up New York nightlife, and reminiscing about other artists who are important to him. With respect to his own work, there are references to Strummer's spliff bunker, his Fender guitar (not a "Stratosphere" but a Telecaster), Yamaha pianos, talking about Errol Flynn with Topper, and the loneliness of working at Electric Lady with "no German girl outside" (a reference to Strummer's girlfriend, Gaby Salter).

As for other artists, Joe references Elvis Presley ("Are you lonesome tonight"), Bo Diddley (with whom The Clash had toured), Buddy Holly, and most interestingly, highly regarded Tex-Mex country artist Joe Ely, who also supported The Clash and with whom Joe hoped to make an album one day.

Detail of Joe's famous battered and be-stickered 1966 Fender Telecaster.

the
Clash

THE SOUND OF THE SINNERS

THE CLASH 4:01

Having already thought better of calling their previous album *The Last Testament*, the band nevertheless discussed naming their new triple album *The Bible*. It would have been a rare religious nod for The Clash, who knock down the doors with "The Sound of the Sinners," a full-blown gospel number on which the band offers yet another song with few previous touchpoints in their catalog, save for, perhaps, the big music of "The Card Cheat" and to a lesser extent "Spanish Bombs."

Willing to wade into debates about religion in interviews of the time, Joe had said that he wanted to get the word "drugs" into a gospel song, and he found a way—through his interest in the idea of people taking so much acid they believe they are Jesus Christ. There's also a whiff of swindling evangelists in the song, with the "holy roller" reference and the faux sermonizing (courtesy of Den Hegerty of UK retro rocker band Darts) massaged in over yet another false ending.

Joe also draws parallels between the story of Jericho being felled with a loud sound and punk music knocking down the social order. Of course, the newly sophisticated Joe felt he had to knock down preconceptions not with rude punk but with a "great jazz note."

Stylistically, the song's Southern Baptist vibe adds to all the record's Americana, with British multi-instrumentalist Tymon Dogg (later of Strummer's post-Clash outfit, the Mescaleros) playing a devotional organ sure to fill the collection plate and Mick strumming along on acoustic while angelic voices sing "judgment day" over and over again (that and too many verses making the song a mite repetitive and long). Fact is, neither the lyrics nor the music are particularly inspired. Besides, for The Clash to cook up a gospel song and stick it on their record veers a little bit into Christ complex itself, somewhat along the lines of thinking they could unveil a worthy triple record a year's time after giving their flock a double.

Weirdly, "The Sound of the Sinners" didn't enter the set list until 1983, at which time it became a regular, even getting showcased at the US Festival, Mick's last gig with the band, where it sounded more like a scrappy electric country spoof by the Replacements or Meat Puppets. Interesting footnote: "The Sound of the Sinners" is purported to be Elvis Costello's favorite Clash song.

OPPOSITE: The Clash knocked down the doors with "The Sound of the Sinners," offering another song with few previous touchpoints in their catalog. New York City, June 25, 1981.

JOE'S SMOKEHOUSE

INSIDE THE INFAMOUS SPLIFF BUNKER

Joe Strummer's famed writing den, known as the spliff bunker, turned out to be useful for more than the fanciful wordsmithing featured all over the sprawl of six sides of *Sandinista!*. In fact, it once saved him from a studio-wide police raid conducted at the hands of some mischievous Blockheads.

"Yeah, Joe's place," laughed Mickey Gallagher, who returned for extensive sessions with the band, both in Electric Lady and Wessex, not to mention the Manchester trip that produced "Bankrobber" and "Broadway." "Every studio that we used to record, the big rooms, they'd put all the equipment in, and the roadie would get all the flight cases and he built like a house." He would pile them up, but you could actually go in it. You'd turn the corner and have a little room in there, open tops, but all the flight cases. But Joe used to just use the flight cases as a desk. While we were recording in the studio, he'd be writing the lyrics in there, and he'd obviously skin up a few. The relaxation creates a bit of that environment. And that was what they called the spliff bunker in the studio. It's his writing place. It got name the name spliff bunker or spliff cupboard later on, but it was essentially that—a little place where he could go and have privacy with his writing pad and his pencils and just sit there and write lyrics while the tracks were being recorded."

"There is a funny story about that," continues Gallagher, referring to an incident that occurred September 10, 1980. "[Ian Dury and] the Blockheads were on *Top of the Pops*, an English chart show, and we decided to dress up in policemen's uniforms. You know, English bobbies, with the helmets with the tips on their heads, sort of thing. And we did the show. We had a song called 'I Wanna Be Straight,' so we dressed as policemen. And after the show, because we put policemen's uniform on, we actually felt powerful. People don't even look at you; you just see a uniform and you turn away. And I love it, but it's very strange. So we walked around the *Top of the Pops* building, BBC, in Shepherds Bush, in these police uniforms, proceeding—because in police uniform, you don't walk, you proceed.

"So I had to go to Wessex after the thing, and I was taking our saxophone player, Davey Payne, to do a session there with The Clash. So we said, 'Let's go up there with the uniforms on' [*laughs*]. So we all piled into my Volvo, which looked like a police car anyway. If we would've been nicked, we would've been banged up for impersonating policemen. We had the police helmets all lined up in the back of the window. We spin right across London, up to Wessex studio, and when we got there, we're all hyped, man, jumped out, 'Let's bust 'em!'

"So we ran in there, and there was some other hippie band recording in the studio. They freaked out—'Up against the wall!'—they just saw all these uniforms piling out of this car. And we ran in and did this whole scenario. I ran into and I arrested Mick Jones, who's walking across the studio. 'You, boy! What you got in your hands?!' He turned around and saw the uniform and he just crumpled into jelly.

"Anyway, this whole thing went off. We went into the booth and arrested the engineers and all sorts of things. And everybody forgot about Joe, who was in the spliff bunker, in the studio. And of course they all recognized us eventually, and it's all, Yeah, yeah, yeah, and we were just relaxing and everything. And of course, you've got Joe in the bunker, peeking out, thinking, 'why are all these policemen all settling in here?' He's sitting in the box with all his gear. So it was good forty-five minutes before, 'Oh, where's Joe?' And of course he's hiding out in there, sitting there laying low."

Another amusing highlight of Gallagher's run with The Clash was having his kids featured as guest vocalists on a couple of previously recorded anthems, reconstituted for *Sandinista!*.

"Yes, that was funny as well," he recalls. "What happened was, I was doing Blockheads sessions from ten in morning, until about nine at night, have a break, and then I would go up and do the sessions at Wessex with The Clash, and I would take my family up. The kids would sleep up there and everything [*laughs*]. I'd just go all night, recording there, come home, get a few hours sleep, and then back to the Blockheads studio. So that went on for quite a while.

"The two boys did 'Career Opportunities,' but what happened with 'Guns of Brixton,' as I say, I was doing a Blockheads session and we were wrapping it up and I was about to go to Wessex to do my night sessions. My family were down at the Blockheads' studio, and I had a little girl, she was four at the time, and she was besotted by Paul [*laughs*], so she knew 'Guns of Brixton,' the verse and the chorus. So before we packed the studio up, she wanted to sing. So the engineer stuck her on a chair with her little legs sticking straight out, big pair of headphones on, and I just started playing the piano. She sang part of 'Guns of Brixton' and then went, 'That's enough now. I'm tired of singing,' and stopped. And I took a cassette of that up to Wessex when I left and played it to Mick Jones, and he said, 'Oh, we gotta have that on the album!' So that's how it got bungled in. It was all creativity, you know what I mean? Weird and wonderful. That's what I liked about The Clash and that's what I like about the business—getting involved in stuff like that [*laughs*]."

THE
CLASH
CBS TRAFFIC

Mickey Gallagher: "Joe used to just use the flight cases as a desk. While we were recording in the studio, he'd be writing the lyrics in there, and he'd obviously skin up a few. The relaxation creates a bit of that environment."

POLICE ON MY BACK

EDDY GRANT 3:16

OPPOSITE: Airport security on my back. The band mugs with guards at JFK Airport upon arriving in New York City for their legendary residency at Bond International Casino.

The closest thing to a clanger worthy of Pete Townshend on the record and it turns out to be a cover, "Police on My Back" being a mild garage-into-psychedelic rocker with good bones from the 1968 *Baby, Come Back* album by North London act the Equals. Famed for their hit song of that name, the Equals' chief songwriter and guitarist was Eddy Grant, who went on to considerable success with pop reggae hit "Electric Avenue," from his seventh solo record, *Killer on a Rampage*, which managed gold in the United States. Paul has said that Mick introduced the band to the Equals' version of the song and that they used to play it on the tour bus.

Once they decided to cook up their own version, it became one of the first numbers attempted for the album, with just Joe, Topper, and Mick (on bass) getting the track down with Mikey Dread producing at their first studio stop, a short-lived visit to The Power Station on West 53rd in New York before they were kicked out and found Electric Lady. Paul, still in Vancouver working on the film *Ladies and Gentlemen, the Fabulous Stains* with Steve Jones and Paul Cook of the Sex Pistols, added his bass parts much later at Wessex back in the UK. Also recorded at The Power Station were covers of "Louie Louie" and Prince Buster's "Madness," nothing for the record having been written at that point (in fact, the band had been toying with the idea of a covers EP or issuing a single every month).

The Clash play the song punchier, faster, and heavier than the original, with the apex being Mick's pained, "What have I done?" Is the exasperated protagonist, who knows there's been a killing, protesting his innocence, or is he lamenting the fact that there's damn good reason for the police to be on his trail seven days a week? It's a clever turn of phrase in its ambiguity.

The signature opening salvo, a very electric guitar as police siren, was in the original too, but live, The Clash seemed to miss the opportunity to open the song with the strong effect. Indeed, in its various live incarnations, the song never quite matched the focused

heat of the studio version, with the band playing it variously too fast, too choppy, or too loose—not surprising, given its performance across the tenure of three different drummers.

It was also a missed opportunity that "Police on My Back" was not chosen for release as a US or UK single, being issued as an A-side only in Australia and as the B-side to "Hitsville U.K." in the United States. However, like many Clash songs, the track lives on in medium rotation on classic rock radio despite a lack of initial push. "Police on My Back" in fact has become, over time, *Sandinista!*'s most enduring and remembered song.

MIDNIGHT LOG

THE CLASH 2:34

The Clash confound again on their guided tour of human nature, set to as many musical genres imaginable. "Midnight Log" sounds storied and traditional, yet still hard to pin. Like a covert crossroads meeting at the witching hour between "The Leader" and "Look Here," the song feels like jazz dressed up as rockabilly, with its quick shuffle beat (high-hat replaced, possibly, by wood block), its harmonica and cocktail piano, and guitar lines and licks dressed up in a leather jacket at the sock hop. There's even a slight nod to reggae, thanks to the mixed-back rhythm guitar strokes on two and four.

Joe's vocal gives a beatnik flair to the proceedings, adding a rap-type quantity of lyrics over the top of what soon starts to feel like a backing track for a late-'50s poetry reading in Greenwich Village. In fact, the lyric is almost film noirish, with devilish thoughts plaguing the opening and closing credits, while in between, friends, spies, government officials, corporations, cops, and lawyers are all up to deceit.

Bond International Casino, May 28, 1981.

THE EQUALISER

THE CLASH 5:46

On the second half of *Sandinista!*, The Clash included dub versions of earlier songs and gave them new names. But with "The Equaliser," they reversed and compressed the formula, beginning a new (but very laid-back) song with a minute or so of a dub version of something yet to come.

Drenched in trippy echo and reverb, plus random sleigh bells and sound effects resembling shots fired in early video games, "The Equaliser" at its core is anchored by a sparse but steady bassline, which, with Topper's light but busy drum track, serves as a bed for a wandering violin of the "Rome is burning" variety from Tymon Dogg. Piano notes echo off the walls as well, as does Mick, who mostly loiters through with muted picking here or there, again, in the spirit of texture practiced by everybody except Paul.

As for the lyrics, Joe is expressing his socialist ideals, even if he grew to realize that the relationship between capitalism and compassion is a complex dance. Strummer's screed is delivered in a sort of dope smoke Rasta reverie, the effect underscored by the echo applied to his vocals, turning them into another crazy house of mirrors instrument at times, as he, like Mick, seems to drift in and out of the session. The imagery is of a plantation worker, whips, slavery, gang bosses, and no escape from the weary drudge across generations. There are also references to specific seats of power beyond the fields and mines, to Geneva, Rome, and Wall Street.

Swinging the song Rasta, in tandem with the dub reggae music and the seemingly tropical vibe of the work regimen described, Joe laments that the simple and natural world as we know it was built by the sweat of exploited workers, who were then told by "the stealers of Zion" that it was not theirs.

"The Equaliser" occupies a space between the album's tighter reggaes and the sense of collapse represented by the dubs. Again, parlor games, but had the band drawn the line here and delivered a double album, it is very likely that *Sandinista!* would be heralded as a second lightning strike, with The Clash following up greatness with a still greater achievement. No one likes a mess—unfortunately, by the band's sixth album, things were destined to get even messier.

THE CALL UP

THE CLASH 5:28

BELOW AND OPPOSITE: "The Call Up" b/w "Stop the World," UK, November 28, 1980. Mick later claimed the song was influenced by debates over conscription in the United States at the time.

Unfortunately, manager Bernie Rhodes' infamous "No more hats" edict, which he levied upon his return to the band in time for *Combat Rock* (he felt headgear distracted from the band in photos), came too late to apply to costumes during the *Sandinista!* period, with the guys looking a little ridiculous in the production video for "The Call Up," issued as the album's ill-advised first UK single in a picture sleeve and backed with the non-LP "Stop the World." The band would also record an instrumental version of the song, "The Cool Out," released on a single with the "The Call Up," "The Magnificent Seven," and an instrumental version of the last called "The Magnificent Dance" (neither of these alternates are exactly "dubs").

Filmed by Don Letts in a Kings Cross warehouse owned by journeyman traditional rock and blues vocalist Chris Farlowe, a military memorabilia collector who also supplied the props, the video portrays the band in full-on political mode, Joe morosely delivering his anti-draft diatribe set to a dark minor-chord funk. Meanwhile, Mick sits on the cab of a truck dressed for safari, while Paul is on an armored car and Topper is kitted out in flight gear.

The song's distinguishing feature from a musical point of view is that the melody is played on xylophone so high up the register that it resembles bells, accompanying reggae down strokes on guitar over an interlocking synthesized and traditional bass riff. Topper supplies an unyielding mid-tempo 4/4 beat while Joe lodges a seemingly halfhearted protest against a powerful war machine, using the same weary, defeated vocal melody over

and over. Answering the call for musicians, Ivan Julian from Richard Hell's Voidoids supplied some guitar work.

There is in fact no chorus, no middle eight, no break, and no variation other than its intro featuring a synthesizer and air raid siren. What results is a sort of fatalistic marching song of five-plus minutes, with soldiers as automatons on a conveyor belt toward certain death.

The reading is reinforced by the inclusion of US Marines hollering, "Hup, two, three, four." Then there's a mention of Kiev and Ukraine's wheat fields, and suddenly the listener wonders if the protagonist is a Soviet conscript lamenting being marched off to war before he's even embarked on his first romance.

Mick has said that the song was influenced by debates over conscription in the United States at the time, remarking that he had even attended a protest on New York's Upper West Side about the issue. Late in the sequence, the Doomsday Clock is referenced, Joe indicating that it's fifty-five minutes past eleven, the Cold War therefore slightly less hot than it would be for Iron Maiden in 1984, when Bruce Dickinson (a real pilot) would glance at his watch and declare it "2 Minutes to Midnight."

29th November, 1980 New Musical Expr

HE CALL UP
w STOP THE WORLD
HE CLASH

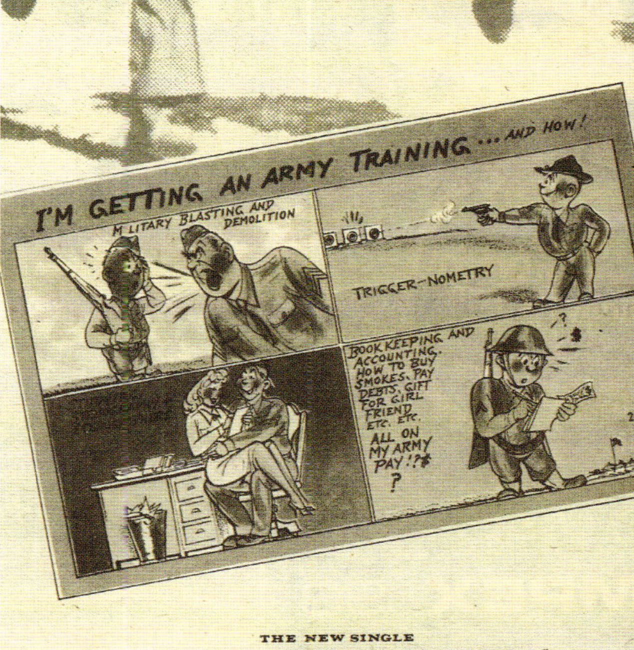

THE NEW SINGLE
"FROM THE FORTHCOMING L.P. "SANDINISTA!"
OUT NOW IN PICTURE BAG

WASHINGTON BULLETS

THE CLASH 5:51

OPPOSITE: Radio Clash Tour, Manchester, UK.

By the time they get to "Washington Bullets," listeners are already aware that The Clash are a political band, but up to now those politics have always tackled one contained and clear-cut concept per song, in the process building a worldview over many tracks. "Washington Bullets," on the other hand, hits listeners with both barrels, Joe challenging us with more names and specifics than usual.

The overarching theme is American imperialism (and attempted American imperialism, as in the case of Cuba), mainly through the pointed image of "Washington bullets," which encompasses both politics imposed from Washington, usually for economic reasons and the suppression of communism but also arms sales representing big revenues for US companies. (Incidentally, Joe claimed to have no idea that Washington's NBA basketball team was called the Bullets.)

And so Joe namechecks Nicaragua, Salvadore Allende and Victor Jara in Chile, Fidel Castro and the Bay of Pigs, violence in Jamaica, Soviets invading Afghanistan, and Chinese oppression against the Buddhists, with the final stanza bringing it all back home in a sense and making note of British bullets, a reminder that the real imperialist pros were Joe's own countrymen, at least before the center of power shifted across the Atlantic.

Joe's action-packed, near checklist of government abuses is set to a pleasant Caribbean rhythm—again, that juxtaposition of heavy lyrics with lilting music—dominated by marimbas tapping out a melody reminiscent of the American folk standard "Turkey in the Straw" over the top of clean R&B guitar lines. Vocals are mostly Joe alone, sometimes Joe in unison with Mick. The vibe is somewhere between "Corner Soul" and "Let's Go Crazy." The song ends with organ swells from Mickey Gallagher, who takes over the song at the end in marked contrast to how deeply buried he is in his other appearances in The Clash's catalog.

Most notable, however, is the fact that the song is nearly the record's title track, with its repeated and climactic chants of "Sandinista," sometimes Joe alone, sometimes Joe and Ellen Foley, sometimes just Ellen. In any event, "Sandinista" was a term Joe had just shouted out during the tracking of the vocals, with Mick instantly picking up on it, suggesting it should be the name of the album.

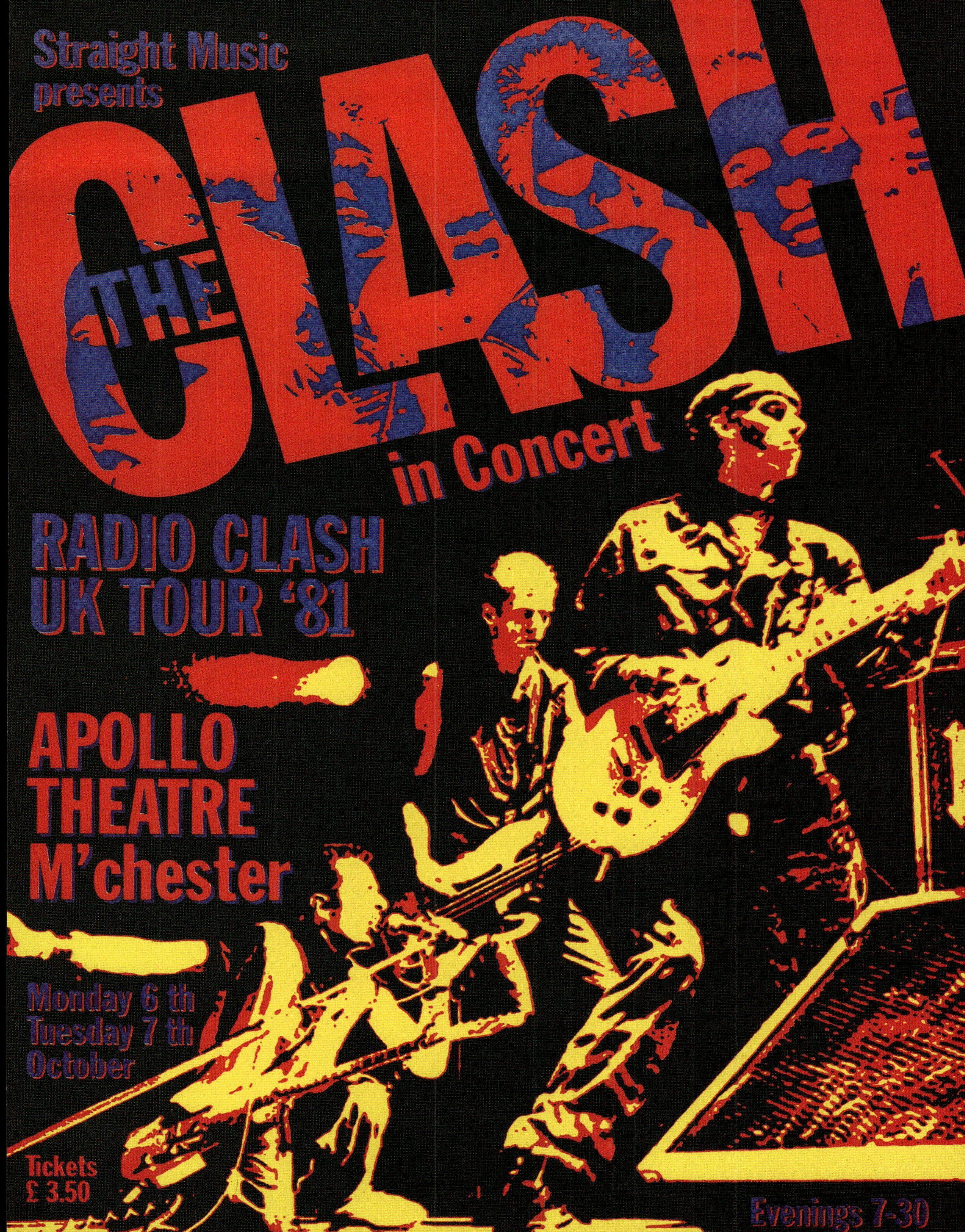
Straight Music
presents
THE CLASH
in Concert
RADIO CLASH
UK TOUR '81
APOLLO
THEATRE
M'chester
Monday 6 th
Tuesday 7 th
October
Tickets
£ 3.50
Evenings 7-30

BROADWAY

THE CLASH 5:48

A jazzy reverie in the spirit of "If Music Could Talk," "Broadway" also roils and swirls, with Mick's guitar offering horn-inspired punctuations. Radio Clash Tour, Lyceum Ballroom, London, October 1981.

A jazzy reverie in the spirit of "If Music Could Talk," "Broadway" also roils and swirls like the Allman Brothers Band or Grateful Dead in jam-band mode, with Mick's guitar evoking the horn-inspired punctuations of Jerry Garcia. Recorded in Manchester at the same sessions that produced "Bankrobber," the song is also an example of The Clash applying their reggae chops to another kind of music, the result being a sort of beat jazz/reggae hybrid essentially written and recorded on the spot with very little planning. Musically, the drums, bass, and piano are most prominent, with guitar in supporting mode as texture.

Over this wistful arrangement, Joe builds the sympathetic story of a guy down and out on the streets, remembering the Depression, recalling a bit of his boxing career, pining at the limos that pull up at bars, and wishing he could get behind the wheel of one and drive the hell out of town. Topper's drum tech Barry "The Baker" Auguste has conjectured that Joe was inspired by a homeless man he often saw sleeping or standing over a heated grate when the band was staying at the Iroquois Hotel in New York City (hence the title, in reference to that city's "Great White Way"), stating that he witnessed Joe pause and ponder the guy one night after returning from the studio at four in the morning.

Also interesting is that, like "If Music Could Talk," Strummer's style is conversational and fragmented; in this instance, he's utilizing the actorly method to evoke the scattered thoughts of a person addled by the cold, the booze, the broken dreams, and other harsh realities of life on the streets.

Apropos of nothing, after the song ends, there's a short hidden track featuring Mickey Gallagher's four-year-old daughter, Marcia, singing "The Guns of Brixton" over a sparse and bouncing piano. Stay tuned for more of this tomfoolery later.

LOSE THIS SKIN

TYMON DOGG 5:07

Underscoring the creative fearlessness of *Sandinista!* is the inclusion of "Lose This Skin," written by violinist Tymon Dogg, an old friend of the band dating back to Joe's busking days. Dogg had moved to New York briefly, working at Folk City on Bleecker Street, and was subsequently summoned down to Electric Lady for a session. The result is a buoyant pop confection swirled with several tracks of Dogg's almost Frippertronic-like tape-looped violin parts, along with a radical vocal from Dogg that yelps and howls somewhere between Feargal Sharkey and David Surkamp from Pavlov's Dog.

Dogg's rapidly sawed violin is placed upon a perky groove of bass and drums, along with very little piano and even less guitar. There's very little Clash-like about the song other than, oddly enough, a melody that one could imagine coming from Mick. In fact, "Lose This Skin" becomes Dogg and Dogg alone as everything drops away for solo violin, which turns out to be a false ending, after which the Big Country–like big music returns for a joyous coda, tinkled with a nice bit of post-punk guitar.

Dogg's inspirational lyric about transformation and escape and new possibilities is a perfect fit to the irresistible and catchy musical track, although its lack of color and flash compared to what Joe might have to say on the same subject is a reminder of how good Joe is at entertaining with words. Still, there are some interesting turns of phrase, such as the reference to Lot's wife, who as the biblical saga goes, looked back at Sodom and was turned into a pillar of salt.

Tymon also released the song as a single in 1981, on Ghost Dance Records, backed with "Indestructible," but did not include it on his subsequent 1982 album, *Battle of Wills*.

Radio Clash Tour, Lyceum Ballroom, London, October 1981.

CHARLIE DON'T SURF

THE CLASH 4:54

Joe's admission that 1979's *Apocalypse Now* made a deep impression on him comes to life on "Charlie Don't Surf," the title of which quotes one of the film's most famous lines, spoken when Colonel Kilgore, played by Robert Duvall, talks about a beach his forces had captured in Vietnam so that his troops could surf, noting that the Vietcong, or "Charlie," don't surf. Napalm is also mentioned in this song (evoking an even more famous line from the movie); it is said that the throbbing synth pattern that opens the song mirrors the sound of the helicopters that open the movie. Joe likened the influence of film on the band and this song to holding a piece of string and finding a song attached to the end of it.

OPPOSITE: London, 1981.

ABOVE: Robert Duvall as Colonel Kilgore on an *Apocalypse Now* promotional poster.

Strummer's oddly imprecise, unpolished lyric seems to touch down most on the idea of imperialism, in this case Americans imposing their will and values—they even think Charlie should learn to surf. Strummer proposes that all of this surety about the American way as the only way can end only in disaster: *Across the world we are going to blow them down*, the Third World onlooker promises. In the meantime, before everybody suffers, the Third World will continue to get stomped, with Africa "choking on their Coca-Cola."

The song's musical structure again finds the band cross-pollinating soft reggae with a traditional music, in this case somewhat of an R&B ballad. Barring the unconnected intro sound effects and some of the outro effects, the arrangement is spare, The Clash core augmented by just a little bit of piano and organ. Mick, however, oscillates between a watery sitar effect and, for his rhythmic reggae slashes, a wave of reverb, while also taking the vocal. The song features another false ending, after which the band shambles into what might be called a short dub version of the song.

An interesting trivia point revolves around the line *Everybody wants to rule the world*. Joe later ran into Tears for Fears' Roland Orzabal in a restaurant and quipped to him that Orzabal owed him a five for nicking the line, to which Orzabal, without a word, produced a five-pound note and gave it to Joe, tacitly admitting his appropriation of the line for the title for his band's No. 1 smash hit.

MENSFORTH HILL

THE CLASH 3:42

A bit disingenuous, isn't it, giving this sound collage an authoritative title like "Mensforth Hill". For what we get here is essentially "Something About England" recorded backward and then gunked up with claustrophobic percolating sound effects and the odd spoken word snippet—call it The Clash's "Revolution 9." Indeed, this is as far as the band would descend into the abstract, even if other forms of sonic loitering are sure to come once we get to *Sandinista!*'s throwaway sixth side.

Did the guys regret padding *Sandinista!*? It depends on who you asked and when. Joe once said that the album was supposed to last the listener a year. Sometimes they'd say it could have and should have been a double; then, if the mood was good, it would be cheerily defended, Mick or Joe particularly cracking that every bit of the record had to be there to make it what it was, which, one supposes, is factually true.

Of note, in the original lyric booklet, this song is designated "Title Theme from Forthcoming Serial."

The Impossible Mission Tour hit 23 European dates from April 27 to May 23, 1981.

JUNKIE SLIP

THE CLASH 2:48

Hard to imagine Topper hearing this and not thinking it was about him as Joe worked his way through a lyric detailing all the telltale signs of a heroin addict putting himself in situations in which slipping up would be inevitable. Topper was in fact in the throes of his addiction, holing up in his hotel room, missing sessions, and winding up in the drunk tank after various wanderings about Manhattan.

There's a comical Keystone Kop vibe to the way the song rolls, or conversely, an eye-winking sense that it's obvious how this dance is going to play out and that it's been the same for time immemorial. First, you find yourself in a bar where the junkies are, and soon you've pawned your coat, car, cigar, guitar, saxophone, and everything from your mom's home.

This sense of inevitability is mirrored in the music's goofy amble down the middle of the train tracks, at the opening fading into what is essentially the closest The Clash ever came to skiffle. Mick's jazzy acoustic minor chords are accompanied by synth bass, handclaps, and Topper all anxious and itchy on brushes, his anxiety matched only by Joe's sense of desperation as he mumbles in a monotone, leaving the listener to wonder exactly who is in trouble here. Adding to the tension, there is no change in melody other than the odd time that things go pear-shaped before corrective measures are taken.

TOP: Tough to imagine Topper, in the throes of addiction, not hearing this song and thinking Joe had penned the lyric about him. New York City, March 7, 1980.

KINGSTON ADVICE

THE CLASH 2:37

OPPOSITE: *Sounds* advert, December 13, 1980.

Side five of *Sandinista!* continues to take shape as a sort of primer for the dub and recycling yet to come on side six, for the last four of side five's six tracks—and for that matter, the first track on side six, "Version City"—feel underwater and cacophonous, three of them sounding like a microphone was placed in the middle of a room with four competing radio stations blaring from the corners. This effect is particularly disconcerting in the context of what would otherwise feel like two perfectly serviceable songs, "Kingston Advice" and "The Street Parade."

The present track, "Kingston Advice," presages Big Audio Dynamite with its noisy mix of reggae, hard rock distortion pedal guitar, and dance groove. The noise comes from sampled videogame sounds, errant guitar skronk, and the echoey underwater effects on the vocals, not to mention Joe's approach to singing the song, which is hectic and exhausted at the same time.

Lyrically, the guys seem like they can't get over the violence and the threat of violence in Jamaica. Two records back, "Safe European Home" addressed the band's first trip there, with the second similarly aborted trip being addressed not too many songs ago, Joe telling us in "Washington Bullets" that "a youth of fourteen got shot down there."

On "Kingston Advice," Joe gets progressively darker about the situation, remarking on how cheap life is, how there's no food but weapons are plentiful, and how it's become easier to settle disputes with a gun rather than talking them through. There's also blame cast at the government, but in the final analysis, Joe sounds defeated, lamenting from the murk that these days he doesn't know what to sing—and even more gravely implying that reality is killing both his will and his ability to make music.

THE NEW CLASH TRIPLE ALBUM 'SANDINISTA' ONLY £4.29 AT VIRGIN

FEATURING THEIR SINGLE 'THE CALL UP'

THOUSANDS OF OTHER SPECIAL OFFERS

ELVIS PRESLEY 40 Greatest Hits (2LP) £4.99
BLONDIE Eat To The Beat £3.99*
Parallel Lines £3.99*
RORY GALLAGHER Irish Tour '74 (2LP) £5.29*
SKIDS Absolute Game £3.99
MAGAZINE Real Life £3.99

SPECIAL OFFERS ON CASSETTES

TALKING HEADS Talking Heads '77 £1.99
CAPTAIN BEEFHEART Shiny Beast £1.99
BOW WOW WOW C30, C60, C90 Go! £1.15

BOOKS & CALENDARS

JIM MORRISON BIOGRAPHY - No One Here Gets Out Alive £3.95
THE CLASH - Before and After £4.50
THE JAM - Modern World by Numbers £3.95
MODS £3.95
THE POLICE - 1981 Calendar £3.45

12" SINGLES

DAVIE BOWIE Ashes to Ashes £2.99
BLONDIE The Tide Is High £2.99
PENETRATION Danger Signs 49p

*Cassette or LP Price

£1.50 TO £2.50 OFF LIST PRICE ON THE VIRGIN TOP 10 ALBUMS

DAVID BOWIE Scary Monsters £2.99
THE JAM Sound Affects £3.39
UB40 Signing Off £2.99*
BARBRA STREISAND Guilty £3.49
BRUCE SPRINGSTEEN The River (2LP) £4.4
KATE BUSH Never For Ever £3.49
FLEETWOOD MAC Live Double £3.99
ORCHESTRAL MANOEUVRES IN THE DARK Organisation £3.49
STEVIE WONDER Hotter Than July £3.49
THE CLASH Sandinista (3LP) £4.29

AT LEAST £1 OFF LIST PRICE ON ALL VIRGIN TOP 11-60 ALBUMS

DEEP PURPLE Live Double £4.79
MAGAZINE Play £2.99
IAN DURY Laughter £3.99
NOT THE NINE O'CLOCK NEWS £3.99*

THOUSANDS OF ALBUMS AT ONLY £1.99 OR LESS

DARTS Amazing Darts 99p
DEREK AND CLIVE Ad Nauseum £1.99
FUNKADELIC One Nation Under A Groove 99p

EDWARD

London Megastore 14 Oxford Street London W1 (Nr. Tottenham
62/64 Kensington High St W8 Tel: 01-937 8587
9 Marble Arch W1 Tel: 01-262 6985
130 Notting Hill Gate W11 Tel: 01-221 6177
Oxford Walk 150/154 Oxford Street W1
Birmingham 74 Bull Street Tel: 021-236 9432.
Brighton 5 Queens Road Tel: 0273 28167
Bristol 12 Merchant Street Tel: 0272 290499
Cardiff 6/7 Duke Street Tel: 0222 390418
Coventry 11 City Arcade Tel: 0203 27579
Croydon 12a Suffolk House George Street
Edinburgh 18a Frederick St. Tel: 031-226 4042
Exeter 92 Queens Street Tel: 0392 57156
Glasgow Megastore 28/32 Union Street Tel: 041-221 0103
Leeds
Liverpool 169 Market Way St. John's Centre Tel: 051-708 0366
Manchester Arndale Centre
Milton Keynes 59 Silbury Arcade Secklow Gate West Tel: 0908 660404
Newcastle 10/12 High Friars
Nottingham 21 Clumber St. Tel: 0602 40096
Plymouth 105 Armada Way Tel: 0752 60435
Sheffield 137 The Moor Tel: 0742 760929
Southampton 16 Bargate Street Tel: 0703 34961
Swansea

THE STREET PARADE

THE CLASH 3:28

Uncharacteristically personal lyrically, "The Street Parade" can be heard as a continuation and expansion of the shiftlessness and helplessness expressed in the song prior. Only now Joe, who has sidelined himself for a period of reflection, is suffering at being left alone with his thoughts. He is desperate in love in the first stanza, desperate with "these crying times" in the second stanza, and expressing spiritual desperation by the third stanza. The curious effect seems to be an erasure of identity. Defiant as Joe wants to be, he still believes he "will disappear into the street parade." Of note, by the late 1980s, Joe found himself suffering with bouts of depression.

Whether the street parade signifies celebration or defeat is open to discussion, and the musical soundtrack to Joe's musings cleverly leaves listeners on the fence. There is a parade-like quality to the cacophony, but one could also see this as a death march. Topper lays down an unyielding beat akin to a stiff shuffle, while Gary Barnacle plays beat jazz sax and both Joe and Mick sing despondently in the distance. Steel drums play mournfully against character as off-kilter and stabbing guitars add further dissonance.

The result is a curious deep album track that's sort of sabotaged before it can become a song, as if thrashing away it's shoved underwater. Nonetheless, the band saw great value in the track, playing it live through 1981 and insisting on its inclusion on the *Clash on Broadway* box set against the label's wishes—like "Train in Vain," it appears as an uncredited hidden final track.

OPPOSITE: Radio Clash Tour, Lyceum Ballroom, London, October 1981.

BELOW: Poster and advert for the band's October 1981 residency at the London Lyceum, October 1981.

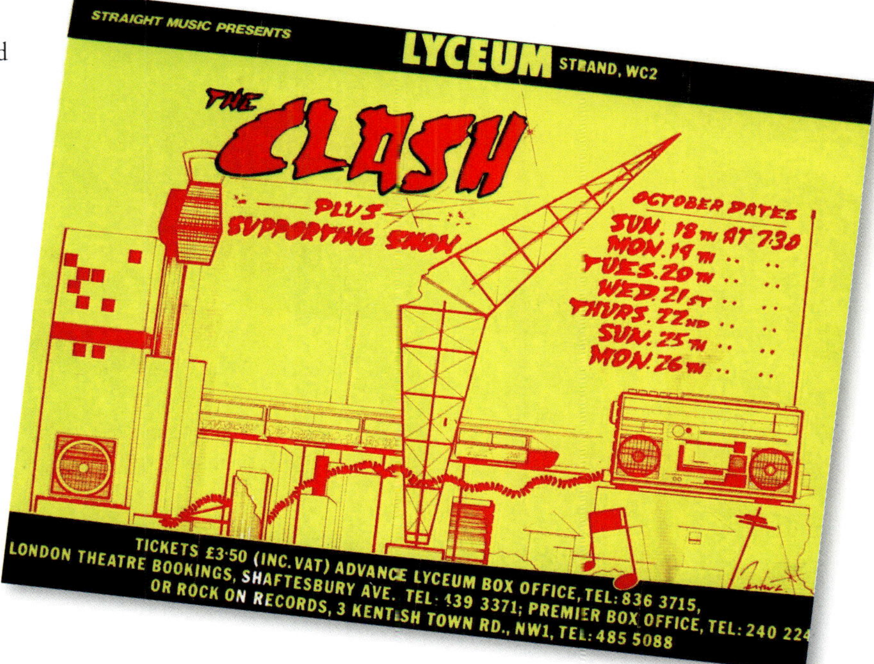

VERSION CITY

THE CLASH 4:21

Sandinista!'s notorious side six begins with some semblance of a real song, although "Version City" is another one of these later tracks on which the band seems to undermine their triple-record mission. Lyrically, it's substantive enough, Joe offering a fresh take on the rock 'n' roll train metaphor. Amusingly, his train travels through Acapella Pass, Gibsontown, Fenderville, and Mesa Boogie Ranch, but to keep it modern, also "straight through Syndrum Inc." (a reference to the synthesizer equivalent of drums, which gained some popularity in the 1980s).

On the musical front, the song is sort of scattershot and funky Memphis soul, featuring a heavy but loose backbeat sprinkled with oblique, jazzy harmonica and piano plus R&B guitar stabs, mostly only on the four. The bluesy and slightly pitchy dual vocal mixed muddy and then sent way back hinders accessibility. Also almost subliminally wrecking the song's chances is the comedic intro (with bookending outro) that sounds like an interlude from a *Monty Python* album.

LIVING IN FAME

DREAD/THE CLASH 4:50

Slightly more than a dub version of "If Music Could Talk," "Living in Fame" is more like a dub but with the bonus of an alternate lyric and vocal by Mikey Dread, who puts up a stoned theory about how bands should live up to their name. The Selecter, the Specials, Madness . . . The Clash. He actually makes some sense to begin, less by the time he gets to Madness—and then there's The Clash, where he's plainly not sure what they should represent.

Then it's as if Dread gives up this train of thought entirely, mixing in Rasta stuff and flying saucers, although he namechecks a few more bands, specifically the Sex Pistols, Generation X, and the Nipple Erectors, Shane MacGowan's first band.

The spirit of dub soon takes over in tandem with the increasingly jamming quality of the vocal. There's reverb all over the sax and occasionally the keys and the palm-muted guitar, and then a sort of percussive rain/scratchy vinyl effect emerges, accompanied by congas. Topper's ambling beat drops out occasionally before Joe wraps it up with a "Fuckin' 'ell, Mikey."

OPPOSITE: Impossible Mission Tour, Milan, Italy, on May 21, 1981.

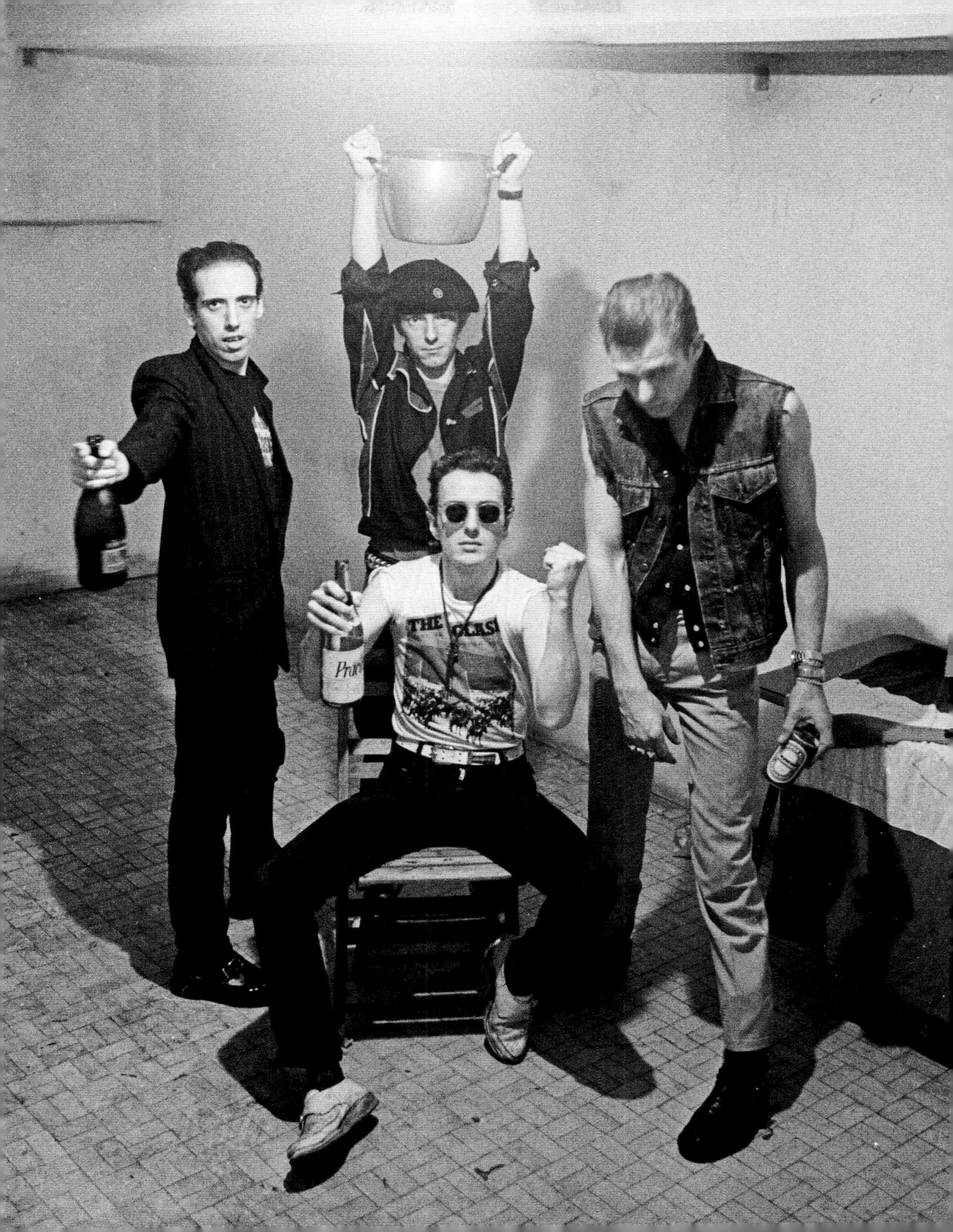

SILICONE ON SAPPHIRE

THE CLASH 4:17

"Silicone on Sapphire" puts the band firmly in dub mode, this one being a very psychedelic take on "Washington Bullets" on which Joe rattles off surprisingly modern computer jargon—modem connecting!—right channel to left and back again in a robot voice upward of eighty times. And he's way back in the mix, buried under a washing, phase-shifting flood of video game and synthesizer sounds. Topper's drums are made trashy (like a Mack mix), but the marimbas are mercifully left alone. The result sounds like a roundtable summit on *Star Trek's* USS *Enterprise*, attended by the likes of Hawkwind, Gong, and Parliament-Funkadelic. Paul most definitely found the exercise pointless, possibly of value only if you smoked enough pot.

VERSION PARDNER

THE CLASH 5:22

Again, dub is treated as a blue smoke that wafts over a Clash song from the spliff bunker, "Version Pardner" beginning like an alternate violin-dominated arrangement of "Junco Partner" until Joe gives up on the vocal to let various quirky sounds have their say. He wanders back in, soon to drift out again with echo, leaving the groove, most consistently consisting of drums, bass, piano, and synth but also various whistle sounds and much reverb applied to everything. All told, this might be the least creative and substantive of the dubs, on par with "One More Dub" but more musical to be sure than "Mensforth Hill."

OPPOSITE: "This Is Radio Clash" b/w "Radio Clash," UK, November 20, 1981. The non-LP "This Is Radio Clash" resulted from the same 1981 recording sessions that gave us "Car Jamming" and "Sean Flynn," both of which would appear on *Sandinista!*'s follow-up, *Combat Rock*. It was released in both 7- and 12-inch formats.

Radio CLASH
VOLUME
POWER
LISBON
PARIS
MOSCOW
ROME
OSLO
NEW YORK
GLASGOW
RADIO CLASH
BERLIN
LONDON
TOKYO
TREBLE
BASS

Radio CLASH
VOLUME
POWER
LISBON
PARIS
MOSCOW
ROME
OSLO
NEW YORK
GLASGOW
RADIO CLASH
BERLIN
LONDON
TOKYO
TREBLE
BASS

Radio CLASH

昭和57年2月1日発行・毎月1回1日発行・第14巻第2号・昭和54年11月27日国鉄首都特別扱承認雑誌4776号・昭和44年6月20日第3種郵便物認可

MUSIC MAGAZINE

ミュージック・マガジン

1982
2

30人の選んだベスト・アルバム 1981

1981発売レコード 全1670枚のリスト

CAREER OPPORTUNITIES

THE CLASH 2:30

OPPOSITE: With a new year and new album on the horizon, the band would close out their *Sandinista!* era and open 1982 by embarking on their only tour of the Far East.

Drawing further comparisons between *Sandinista!* and the circus that was *The Great Rock 'n' Roll Swindle*, The Clash dare to include an easy-listening version of their debut album's "Career Opportunities," here sung by keyboardist Mickey Gallagher's two boys, Luke and Ben, with the odd lyric change, no less, to put it more in their realm of experience. Pleasant enough, the song also fuels frustration, first, for being a redo and, second, for being sung by someone outside the band in close sequencing proximity to lead vocal cameos by Mikey Dread and Tymon Dogg.

To poke and provoke buyers further, the arrangement is wildly un-Clash-like (granted, not that we have a handle anymore at this point), essentially put together like children's music, the tempo reduced to a relaxed recline, Gallagher playing harpsichord along to an acoustic guitar strummed with good cheer. Where you should sequence something like this featuring kid vocals (if you must include it at all) is anyone's guess, but in and among a side otherwise obscured by dope smoke seems to warrant a distress call to child welfare services.

SHEPHERDS DELIGHT

DREAD/THE CLASH 3:29

Sandinista! ends in a comfortable if curious manner with a quiet lie-down of an instrumental that sounds like a lost reggae B-side from *The Gospel According to the Meninblack* by The Stranglers—the first time I heard it, I thought these little squeaks 'n' shrieks were made by the very same witchy hags. This music emerged from the Manchester sessions with Mikey Dread, noted for producing "Bankrobber," the pre-*Sandinista!* single that almost served as a jumping-off point for the massive album to come.

There's a bit of "Mensforth Hill" to "Shepherds Delight," given the intrusive spoken-word muddle, including at the end—"Could it really happen?" "I hope not"—which transitions into the same frightening missile launch sound effect sampled in that infuriating work of *musique concrète*. Here, however, the roar of war is left unadorned and extended, putting a deep stab of an exclamation point on the gradual descent into madness represented by the fifth side's collapse and absorption into the nihilistic and terminating side six.

★THE CLASH★COMBAT

SIDE 1

KNOW YOUR RIGHTS

CAR JAMMING

SHOULD I STAY
OR SHOULD I GO

ROCK THE CASBAH

RED ANGEL DRAGNET

STRAIGHT TO HELL

SIDE 2

OVERPOWERED BY FUNK

ATOM TAN

SEAN FLYNN

GHETTO DEFENDANT

INOCULATED CITY

DEATH IS A STAR

Recorded at Ear Studios, London, and Electric Lady Studios, New York City

Release Date
May 14, 1982 (UK: CBS FMLN 2 and US: Epic FE 37689)

Made by The Clash
Recorded by Joe Blaney and Jerry Green
Tape operator Eddie Garcia
Mixed by Glyn Johns

RIAA Certification: 2x platinum
Top Position: No. 7

COMBAT ROCK

JOE STRUMMER
Vocals, Guitar,
Harmonica, Piano

MICK JONES
Vocals, Guitar, Keyboards

PAUL SIMONON
Vocals, Bass

TOPPER HEADON
Drums, Piano, Bass

GUESTS:
Tymon Dogg, Piano
Tommy Mandell, Keyboards
Gary Barnacle, Saxophone
Allen Ginsberg, Futura 2000,
Ellen Foley, Joe Ely, and
Kosmo Vinyl, Vocals

Stick around long enough, stick your neck out far enough—in rock or in any business—and strange things can happen—maybe even good things. Such is the author's view of *Combat Rock*, the album that was a hit despite itself.

Actually, *Combat Rock* shifted units for the most insipid of reasons: it had a couple of hit singles, each of the equally insipid novelty type, one of them conceivable as a hit and the other just as oblique and spare and unlikely a hit as a half-dozen other tracks on the album exhibiting shades of *Sandinista!* (a jaunty and playful video embraced by MTV didn't hurt either).

But the existence of *Combat Rock* (if not its commercial success) and the trajectory toward it made some sort of screwy sense nonetheless. The band found themselves back at Electric Lady, reliving the exciting first sessions for *Sandinista!* and soaking up the experience of white-knuckle New York, not much having changed since their last time there. Mick was staying with girlfriend Ellen Foley while the rest of the band camped out at the Iroquois Hotel in Midtown—one particular attraction was the fact that James Dean used to stay there and even get his hair cut at the shop just off the lobby, prompting Paul and Joe to go there as well.

The music cooked an' cocked up for the album reflected a further shift from one black music (reggae) to another. Mick and Joe chose to explore hip-hop, funk, and dance along with a futuristic take on dub, which they applied to all of it—the "it" including about as many passing nods to rock as there were last time out, as well as a diminished but still present slice of reggae, albeit of a deconstructed type.

But unlike last time, where the band kept *everything*, this time the eighteen resulting tracks became the subject of intense debate. Joe, along with a returning and shit-stirring Bernie Rhodes (who had left the band in 1979 and retuned in 1981 at Joe's insistence), and to some extent Paul, wanted to pare the material down to a single record, whereas Mick wanted to fill things out with a full capitulation to a dance mix vibe. For his part, Topper found himself descending further into cocaine and heroin addiction and would be sacked in due time. Unresolved after the December 1981 sessions, the band went on a Far East tour between January and March 1982, returning

to have Glyn Johns, at the behest of Bernie Rhodes, resolve the issue. Collaborating with Mick and Joe, Johns took the record down from Mick's seventy-seven minute mix to a forty-six–minute single album.

The resulting record retained a fair bit of Mick's dance-mix vibe, albeit applied to songs with slower tempos than typically associated with traditional urban dance music. Cinematic snippets, spoken-word samples, and other quirks of ear candy were everywhere, resulting in a record that, again, challenged commercial sensibilities in the same manner as the songs on *Sandinista!* that were considered indulgent. If the sonics were thorny and brittle yet bright, Joe matched the fearlessness of the music with example after polemic example of political lyrics as dense as "Washington Bullets" and then some.

But never underestimate the public. *Combat Rock*, pretty much carted on the donkey backs of "Should I Stay or Should I Go" and "Rock the Casbah," wound up platinum in the United States by January 1983 (achieving double platinum in 1995), while reaching No. 7 on *Billboard* and No. 2 on the UK charts. What's more, it was a song by Topper, who, completely against type, wrote and then played piano and drums on "Rock the Casbah," which was embraced in America as the album's biggest hit, reaching No. 8 and eventually status as the band's most enduring track of all time.

Combat Rock reflected a further shift from one black music (reggae) to another, with Mick and Joe choosing to explore hip-hop, funk and dance, along with a futuristic take on dub. World Music Festival, Bob Marley Centre, Kingston, Jamaica, November 27, 1982.

KNOW YOUR RIGHTS

THE CLASH 3:40

OPPOSITE: Joe goes straight for the jugular on "Know Your Rights" (*all three of them—ha!*).

BELOW: "Know Your Rights" b/w "First Night Back in London," UK, April 23, 1982.

Given what's to follow, it seems almost an act of cynical deception to kick off *Combat Rock* with what amounts to its fastest, most guitar-driven, and heaviest song, if not exactly its most conventional.

A bit of the ol' Adverts' 1978 track "One Chord Wonders" contributes to this one, as Joe rants over what is essentially a beat made of one chord, with no chorus, although there is a transitional segment. Still, the song-framing chordal stabs recall the punkified reggae of "London Calling." As well, there's a bit of a rockabilly feel to the frantic beat and some of the reverb and muted guitar effects, and then, as if to underscore the retro, a spaghetti Western–influenced solo (Mick had produced Theatre of Hate's *Westworld* at Wessex in August 1981, just before the Freston Road sessions). Ultimately, the urgency of the final track was indeed the cause of arguments, with Paul wanting more of a reggae feel, inspired by Prince Buster's "Ten Commandments."

Over this hasty construct—less hasty when it comes to the arrangement, which includes piano and effects—Joe goes straight for the jugular in describing how a person's rights (*all three of them—ha!*) come with sabotaging contingencies controlled by the hand of the corrupted powers that be. The shouty vocal melody and phrasing supports Joe's attention-grabbing "This is a public service announcement" opener, as does the one-chord structure—"Know Your Rights" is a document to be read, not a song to be sung, and read perhaps over the clank of the assembly line that this musical track resembles. Police brutality, limits on protest, and onerous stipulations on welfare are all promised by the narrator (perhaps some sort of government drone sent out to address the rabble), but in the end, the only thing left to say is a panicked admonishment to "Get off the streets!"

"Know Your Rights," a product of the early Ear Studio sessions in London and some mixing work on the Far East tour, was issued as a single in the United Kingdom (backed with the non-LP "Last Night in London") three weeks in advance of the album's launch date. It reached No. 43 on the charts—not a great result, but then again that's not bad for something so darn hookless, isn't it?

IGNORE
ALIEN

CAR JAMMING

THE CLASH 3:58

Spare, awkward, and open of architecture, “Car Jamming” finds the band sacrificing music for lyrics, under the influence of hip-hop, which had just barely been invented by this point. Ear to the ground as always, though, The Clash absorb and then reflect the sound of the street. The result is Joe’s most vibrant, livid, and expressionist rap yet, one far beyond “The Magnificent Seven,” oblique, baffling but impressively poetic, and in the aggregate reflective of the whirlwind of gritty activity on the streets of New York at the time.

OPPOSITE: “Car Jamming” reminds one of the famous images of Joe riding tall in a convertible. Here the band leaves Philadelphia’s JFK Stadium where they supported The Who on September 25, 1982.

On the musical tip, the listener is quickly sent into the stoned zone, the dark side of *Sandinista!*, with Topper tapping out a minimal tribal rhythm, augmented by tambourine and later shakers. Mick is relegated to texture, as he often is on *Combat Rock*, on this second song in a row without a chorus. There’s thin and reedy chicken-scratch funk guitar mixed back, as well as a Robert Fripp–like looped Frippertronic drone. Neither matter too much, other than to direct focus toward Strummer’s disorienting, dystopian imagery.

It’s unsurprising that the song came from the same very early sessions that resulted in “This Is Radio Clash” and the atmospheric “Sean Flynn.” All are of a daring suite of songs that seem to be anchored in conventional songwriting and then put through a dub process on the spot, whereas on *Sandinista!* listeners might have been presented with two versions.

As alluded to, the Allen Ginsberg–like lyrics make up for the lack of musical ambition. From the enigmatic title, one gets the image of Joe watching life on the street from a traffic jam but also that he perhaps is adding to the cacophony of radio sounds alluded to twice with his own mobile system blaring, perhaps in part to drown out the din and cognitive dissonance. One is reminded of the famous image of Joe sitting tall in a convertible, snapping shots with a camera—he sees gorillas, hyenas, snakes, a Vietnam vet (The Clash played a 1979 benefit in Cleveland for a vet named Larry McIntyre who had lost both his legs in the war), bankers, ad executives, drug addicts, the ragged standing in bags, and possibly Lauren Bacall. There is no city zoo, so all of this spills onto the sidewalks as Joe contemplates a metropolis on the edge of complete collapse.

SHOULD I STAY OR SHOULD I GO

THE CLASH 3:06

Sort of hard rock and retro rocker at the same time, "Should I Stay or Should I Go" unsurprisingly became a smash single, and it was in fact built to be "a classic," the band remarking that it's the kind of music that they loved to play in rehearsals. Said to be inspired by Mitch Ryder's "Little Latin Lupe Lu," its chords are stacked in the tradition of many old garage rock anthems, including "The Witch" by the Sonics. The song is positively gleeful, from its whacking drums to the pregnant pauses to the evangelical rave-up in the chorus. There's the spirit of punk, the big stacked chords of stadium rock, and, weirdly, a kind of rockabilly vibe like the Cramps but brighter.

"Should I Stay or Should Go?" b/w "Cool Confusion," Europe, June 10, 1982.

Mick, who sings the song as a character amusingly discombobulated, demurred at suggestions that the song, with its amusingly simple-minded lyric, was about his tumultuous relationship with Ellen Foley or his crumbling relations with the band resulting from burnout, Topper, and arguments over the album, saying that it was meant to be a sort of universal world-beater. Still, depending on the interview, he at times copped to all of the above, and Joe did indeed jokingly pen a line (unused) about Mick's tendency to "whinge" (complain) when the crew went on a binge. One of Mick's big complaints was how his vision for *Combat Rock*, a double with longer versions of songs and a dancier overall feel, was usurped by Bernie Rhodes, Clash associate Kosmo Vinyl, Strummer (he called Mick's version a "home movie mix"), and cleanup producer Glyn Johns.

Specific to this track, original suggestive line "around the front or on your back" was switched at the insistence of Johns to the radio-friendly "if you want me off your back." Also on the lyrical tip, Joe and Tex-Mex rocker buddy Joe Ely yell out a bunch of Spanish bits on the song, with an assist from Electric Lady engineer Eddie Garcia, who called his mother to provide an Ecuadorian slant to the final wording. In any event, the spirited Spanish, along with a pile of hootin' and hollerin', couldn't help but stir enthusiasm for the song.

Thus a career-revitalizing anthem was spawned, getting rushed out as a single and then reissued in various permutations and territories, and getting a further slingshot with the release of a live version from Shea Stadium and accompanying video. It was reissued as a single again in 1991, prompted by its use in a Levi's ad campaign, hitting No. 1 in the UK charts and selling more than a million copies. It then garnered further attention in 1999 as a highlight on the *From Here to Eternity* live album and now sits lodged in classic radio playlists.

'Should I Stay or Should I Go?" b/w "First Night Back in London," United States, June 10, 1982.

Lochem Festival, Openluchttheater, Holland, May 20, 1982.

FLYING UNDER THE RADAR

THE CLASH CHIP IN ON ELLEN FOLEY'S *SPIRIT OF ST. LOUIS*

Whether "Should I Stay or Should I Go" relates the story of Mick's tumultuous relationship with New York singer Ellen Foley is up for debate, but Ellen indeed figures into the Clash story quite substantially, providing backup vocals on *Combat Rock* and *Sandinista!* and, most prominently, lead vocals on "Hitsville U.K."

But perhaps the most interesting connection is the presence of all four Clash members on Foley's second album, 1981's *Spirit of St. Louis*, along with the likes of Tymon Dogg, Mickey Gallagher, Norman Watt-Roy, Davey Payne, Bill Price, and Jeremy Green. The album was recorded at Wessex during a break in the *Sandinista!* sessions. The liner notes indicate it was produced by "My Boyfriend," and it features fully six Strummer/Jones compositions among its twelve tracks, three others being written by Tymon.

"It was kind of a big stew," laughed Foley, famed for singing on Meat Loaf's "Paradise by the Dashboard Light" as well as her subsequent acting career. "I was over there and pretty much got caught up with their music and Mick Jones's ideas. The record company wasn't particularly happy about it [*laughs*]. I guess I got caught up in The Clash style and we sort of went ahead and did the record," she said. "Didn't really pay any mind to the record company, which was pretty fun. Sam Lederman, one of the Cleveland International guys [the label that released Meat Loaf's *Bat Out of Hell*], came over to London to hear it and he liked it, so we were fine. Subsequently, when the record came out, they didn't like it so much. But it was kind of an autonomous thing. We just said, 'Yeah, this is what we're gonna do.' That kind of attitude."

Despite the credits, *Spirit of St. Louis* sounds very little like The Clash, testimony to the versatility of the band. Contrasting the album with her debut, Foley said, "*Night Out* was bombastic, with an Ian Hunter/Mick Ronson/Phil Spector kind of sound. That was the position I was coming from, and then it took a big turnaround into European cabaret style, which was a whole different thing. But it was a very familial situation. Everybody I think was in a pretty good place at that period, including Topper—what a great musician. Who knows if they were

LEFT: Mick mixes Ellen Foley's *Spirit of St. Louis* with Mick Ronson (left) and Ian Hunter (right). Ronson and Hunter had collaborated with Foley on her 1979 debut, *Night Out*.

looking at me like, 'Well, give me money to work on this chick's record!' But you know, I don't think so. I think it was fun for them. They'd just been working on *Sandinista!* for such a long time and here they were able to do something different—very different."

Asked if she was surprised they could write such traditional pop music, Foley figured, "No, they had proven themselves. They started out a straightforward punk band but then worked with so many different influences in their music. They had a starting point, and then they became so much more sophisticated than other punk bands that sort of stayed where they were. So, no, I wasn't surprised. That's what they liked to do, and they were completely capable of that."

The songwriting process, however, caught Foley off-guard. "Yes, well, as a solo artist, I hadn't experienced what a band process was quite as much. I was surprised how songs came together in an improvisational, organic way. Different than the way I had worked before. To able to mind-meld and out comes a song—it all just happened," she said. "Their music was so 'in the moment' in terms of what was going on in the world. In that respect, none of these songs had been slated to be Clash songs. I don't think that they would have a song that they would say, 'Yeah, we'll put this out in two years.' I know nothing that was on my record would've been on a possible Clash release."

Spirit of St. Louis reached No. 57 on the UK charts but didn't rank at all back home in the United States, a disappointment to all involved. "You know, if there had been support for the record when it came out, I think 'Torchlight' could have been a hit," reflected Foley. "That marimba sound on there, I think is a very emotional sound. And that is a duet between me and Mick. And the song ["The Death of the Psychoanalyst of Salvador

Dali"] is just so cool. Joe, who was very generous and giving, brought that crazy, surreal lyric—he's basically chief lyricist on the album. And 'My Legionnaire' was actually the Edith Piaf song, so as I say, that was kind of my Edith Piaf period."

Foley's relationship with Mick persisted through the *Combat Rock* sessions. Mick stayed with her while the rest of the band camped out at the Iroquois Hotel. Ellen was around for the famous live stand at Bonds International Casino in Times Square and witnessed the band soaking up even more influence, inspiration that was poured into *Combat Rock.*

"I remember being down there," recalled Foley, asked about Electric Lady. "I remember Mick hanging out with Fab 5 Freddy, because he was very much like a sponge. Obviously, he was into reggae, but also very much these other different cultural kinds of music. Allen Ginsberg showed up one day. That was fun. He came down with his boyfriend, Peter Orlovsky. He was very much into Joe and the poetry and the whole scene. They were hanging out. The whole cross-cultural experience of the band at that time was something very cool to witness."

ROCK THE CASBAH

THE CLASH 3:42

Alas, poor Topper's moment in the Saharan sun arrived just before he was sacked, having worked solo in the studio on the music and subsequent bass, drums, and obstinately hooky piano frame of what would become The Clash's biggest hit ever. The happy incident took place at Electric Lady in New York, although Topper says that it was the product of a band fragmenting, not showing up to work at the same and proscribed times. In this instance, he arrived at two in the afternoon, with the rest not straggling in until about seven in the evening, by which time Topper had banged together a song.

Upon hearing the music, the band thought it needed only minor additions, namely guitar and some additional percussion, mostly bongos, from Topper, as well as a doubling in length. In addition, Joe summarily and literally crumpled up and tossed Topper's boy/girl lyrics with a withering "How incredibly interesting." Joe, deciding to work what became the title phrase into a song, tucked into the bathroom and knocked off new lyrics in less than an hour.

The song tells the story of the banning of rock music after Iran's Islamic Revolution in 1979, with specific reports reaching the West of one unlucky infidel being flogged for owning a disco album. Things don't go well in the song, with the Bedouins rocking out to their "electric camel drum" in their fortress casbah as soon as the authorities are out of earshot. Party in full swing, the king orders his pilots to bomb the casbah square, with the pilots subsequently refusing, tuning the music into their cockpits instead. "The king told the boogie men, 'You have to let that raga drop,'" is a sly reference to the return of Bernie Rhodes, who had bemoaned the jamminess and the length

Topper's moment in the sun arrived just before he was sacked, having concocted the music, including the ridiculously hooky piano frame, for what would become The Clash's biggest hit ever. Lochem Festival, Openluchttheater, Holland, May 20, 1982.

"Rock the Casbah" b/w "Longtime Jerk" and bonus sticker insert, UK, June 11, 1982.

of the band's recent material, most pointedly "Sean Flynn" (see page 204), comparing it to Indian raga music.

Typical of *Combat Rock* songs, "Rock the Casbah" received a coating of sound effects, including early video game samples and a wheedly electronic sample of the song "Dixie," lifted from the alarm on Mick's wristwatch.

A catchy, guilty pleasure—Jones thought it was too comedic to release as a single—the song also benefited in the charts from its goofy video and subsequent high rotation on the suddenly very popular MTV, at that point just coming on line and mesmerizing the United States with a constant churn of first-wave rock videos. With Austin, Texas, standing in for the Middle East in the video, a stereotypical Arab and Jew are seen vamping to the song as the band, highly costumed, mimes the track in front of an oil well, with Terry Chimes by now replacing Topper and Mick covering his face, reportedly because he was in a surly mood.

As an interesting footnote, the former band members were reportedly horrified to learn that American pilots had taken up the song as a sort of anthem in the Gulf Wars.

RED ANGEL DRAGNET

THE CLASH 3:46

Befitting the band's fascination with New York City, "Red Angel Dragnet" pays tribute to the Guardian Angels, a citizen patrol group originally set up in 1979 to help prevent crime on the New York subway system. Here the band, including new old drummer Terry Chimes, catches a Checker in the Big Apple sometime in 1983.

Paul Simonon returns for another lead vocal, on a track that is very much akin to his first vocal turn in the catalog, *London Calling*'s "The Guns of Brixton," insomuch as both are about urban violence. But this time out, befitting the band's fascination with America and specifically New York City that first reared its head on *Sandinista!*, "Red Angel Dragnet" pays tribute to the Guardian Angels, a citizen patrol group originally set up in 1979 to help prevent crime on the New York subway system. The organization's distinct red berets became a media sensation, sparking debate about the role of vigilantes in crime prevention.

Law enforcement resented their presence, and the song brings up a specific incident from December 29, 1981, in which Guardian Angel Frank Melvin was shot and killed by police in Newark under suspicious circumstances, some saying it was crossed wires at a burglary scene and others saying it was intentional.

The need for someone to help the NYPD rescue a city still recovering from its nadir, represented by 1977's blackout and Son of Sam serial killer, is underscored by the edited lift of Travis Bickle's righteous and foreboding monologue from Martin Scorsese's *Taxi Driver* (1976), here sneered and smeared onto the track by Kosmo Vinyl. Paul asks point blank: "Did anyone prophesize these people? Only Travis." Of course reinforcing the theme, Joe adopted the Bickle uniform and Mohawk, while Mick could be seen wearing a Guardian Angel–like uniform complete with army boots and beret—combat rock indeed.

Further tying the song to *Taxi Driver* is a prostitution subtheme, with Paul referencing Jack the Ripper and his killing of the "birds of night" in the darkened alleys of Victorian London. The references to "Not even five enforcement agencies, Not even bobbies on bicycles 2x2," and "Never mind the people" all allude to the idea that the cops are outnumbered and outgunned by criminals. The closing lyrical jam echoes, albeit more vaguely, the drift of *Taxi Driver* and indeed Bickle's drift into madness.

Joe quipped that Paul must have thought that Strummer himself had gone mad. When penning the lyric, Joe ran out of paper back at the Iroquois Hotel and had to write the lyric on a hotel envelope, noting that he had to ring around the edge of it three times to get it all in. Subsequently, Paul had to rotate the envelope to read it.

Unsurprisingly, Simonon puts his typically shouty vocal atop a form of hepped-up reggae, "Red Angel Dragnet" being a face-forward funky construct that gamely follows perhaps Topper's most complicated drumbeat among his Clash work. Admirably, all over *Combat Rock* and a good half-dozen songs on the previous album, the band absorbed underground street music in New York City and then processe it with a reggae flavor that was being incubated back home by The Clash and a variety of punk and post-punk interpreters, such as the Slits and Madness. "Red Angel Dragnet" is a prime example, as well as a solid piece of the album's thematic thrust, with its airy architecture and hip-hop–influenced spoken-word approach.

TOP: Casbah Club USA Tour, Asbury Park, New Jersey, second of a two-night stand, May 30, 1982.

ABOVE: Kosmo Vinyl sneers the famous Travis Bickle monologue from Taxi Driver across "Red Angel Dragnet."

THE
SOUND
REUNION

STRAIGHT TO HELL

THE CLASH 5:26

The product of a frantic last-minute effort to cram in as much music-making at Electric Lady as possible before the band was scheduled to fly to Tokyo to begin a short tour, "Straight to Hell" turned out to be one of *Combat Rock*'s most admired tracks, subsequently issued with "Should I Stay or Should I Go" as a double A-side single, although it has not entered the lexicon of pop consciousness in the same manner as its single partner.

The quiet and contemplative musical track finds Topper tapping out a bossa nova beat on rims and high-hat to a guitar line that Mick had hanging around for a while, Headon musing that one couldn't play rock 'n' roll to what Mick had written. Topper then suggested Joe play along by hitting the bass drum with a lemonade bottle wrapped in a towel, an effect that holds the skittery song together. The original version was nearly seven minutes long and featured longer and more atmospheric instrumental passages, more violin, and an extra verse addressing the Puerto Rican experience in the Lower East Side neighborhood of Alphabet City.

Lyrically, "Straight to Hell" is another fine example of Joe combining disparate vignettes or narratives under a unifying banner, this one being the disposability of human lives. The opening verse talks about the death of heavy industry in the United Kingdom and the attendant job loss, with a subtle tie-in to the fact that, in the end, immigrants are the fuel spent in the firing of the mills. Joe then pivots to children fathered and then subsequently abandoned by American soldiers in Vietnam (though of Japanese origin, the honorific *san* became commonly used by Americans in that conflict). Notably, Coca-Cola is once again mentioned as a symbol of Western imperialism, or at least presence, in developing nations. Joe rounds out the song with a look at drugs in the United States and the immigrant experience in general, reflecting that, as he noted on the round-the-world-tour the band had just completed, "it could be anywhere."

Strummer had fond memories of the recording sessions that produced "Straight to Hell," which was among the band's last work at Electric Lady. Joe recalled the satisfaction of completing a Clash classic after staying up at the Iroquois Hotel the previous night to pen the lyric and then finishing his vocal at twenty minutes to midnight on New Year's Eve. He remembered next taking the E Train from the studio in the East Village back to the vicinity of his hotel and emerging onto Times Square, stuffed with "a hundred billion people."

OPPOSITE: Taking a break at the famed Hitsville U.S.A. Motown Museum, Detroit, Michigan, August 1982.

ABOVE: The double A-side single featuring "Should I Stay or Should I Go" and "Straight to Hell (Edit)," UK, September 17, 1982.

OVERPOWERED BY FUNK

THE CLASH 4:52

"Overpowered by Funk" finds The Clash delving further into New York City's nascent hip-hop scene, which by this point featured funk music and early forms of rap, a style already explored by The Clash on "The Magnificent Seven" and "This Is Radio Clash." The exploration is underscored by the inclusion of a rap by New York graffiti artist Futura 2000, who had done graffiti backdrops live on stage with the band during their stand at the Lyceum in Paris, after which he would take the mic and perform a rap known as "The Escapades of Futura 2000." The collaboration was very much in the spirit of mixed-media performance so associated with the city and Andy Warhol.

An additional performance came from session keyboardist Tommy Mandell (most associated with Bryan Adams), billed as Poly Mandell, who along with Futura 2000, added his part to the basic track that the band had recorded back in London at the People's Hall in Freston Road in September 1981 using the Rolling Stone Mobile.

Unlike early funk experiments by the band, this one fully embraces the '80s, rattling and clattering like Rick James and Prince, livening up *Combat Rock* considerably but also further annoying the old guard.

Stuffed full of words, much like "The Magnificent Seven," "Overpowered by Funk" has Joe proscribing a dose of funk against the world's ills while Futura 2000 (today known simply as "Futura") explains his credo, with the tacit message being that what he does with a spray can is also a form of funk. "I paint on civilization," he proclaims in parallel to Joe's calls for funking out in response to any of about a dozen obstacles life can throw one's way.

Terry Chimes at Hitsville U.S.A. Motown Museum, Detroit, Michigan, August 1982.

ATOM TAN

THE CLASH 2:27

Not heavy, not fast, and nowhere near punk, "Atom Tan" nevertheless rolls like a proper Clash rock song thanks to Topper's spirited snare work (including flams and single-stroke rolls), a dose of bongos, Mick's sexy funk guitar, and Joe and Mick's (friends and fighters in equal measure, although by now tipping toward the latter) flashy call-and-response lyric with Mick dishing that thick South London accent. There's also a pleasurable amount of plush Mick melody, in stingy supply on this improbable hit album, especially come chorus time, like the very best of Big Audio Dynamite.

Lyrically, Joe seems to immerse the listener in a pressure cooker of an urban newscast, business as usual downtown, with references to Batman and the Lone Ranger to boot. The curious title phrase is never made explicit. The obvious image is a nuclear bomb—or is the tan the result of being nervously glued to the TV, voyeuristically peering in on the next motorcycle crash?

Whatever the case, one can only imagine that with a less oblique lyric, "Atom Tan" might have served as a third hit on an album otherwise very barren of radio-friendly songs.

Advert for the canceled spring 1982 shows. Manager Bernie Rhodes intended to send Joe "missing" for a few days to drum up publicity, but Joe went AWOL in Paris, allegedly running the Paris Marathon, no less, and forcing outright cancellation of the dates.

The rift grows . . .

212-HD
& THE BLOCKHEADS
157 W. 57TH STREET
NEW YORK, N.Y.

SEAN FLYNN

THE CLASH 4:30

Sean Flynn was the ex-actor and son of Errol Flynn who gave up film to become a photojournalist. Best known for his work in the Vietnam War, in 1970 he and fellow photojournalist Dana Stone were kidnapped by communist guerillas and never seen again.

Written at Vanilla Studios and recorded at Marcus in April 1981, "Sean Flynn" was not only one of the earliest compositions slated for *Combat Rock* but also one of the most ambitious.

Joe revisits Southeast Asia in this elegy of sorts for the son of actor Erroll Flynn, Sean himself being an actor who retired from the profession at a very young age to become a highly respected combat photojournalist. Producing enduring images of the Vietnam War for the likes of *Time* magazine and UPI, Flynn and war correspondent Dana Stone were riding motorcycles on Highway 1 in Cambodia from Phnom Penh to Saigon when they were kidnapped in a Vietcong ambush on April 6, 1970, and never seen again. According to CIA intelligence, the Khmer Rouge likely executed them in 1971.

In eulogizing Flynn, Joe adds lyrics that reflect his own interest in the Vietnam War and the film *Apocalypse Now*. In fact, the atmospheric and exotic musical track feels like it could soundtrack Captain Willard's trip up the river to execute Kurtz. Topper provides Asian-inflected percussion, while Mick plays chromatic guitar lines with a repeat effect. Gary Barnacle pops in again, drifting in and out with a sax solo while a fluttery flute line further helps create the mood of a peaceful jungle that's concealing silent killers. Also noteworthy is the fact that Pennie Smith, she of *London Calling* fame, shot the album's cover during a tour stop in Southeast Asia, specifically Thailand.

In its original form, "Sean Flynn" was nearly eight minutes long; in its final state, it was just over four minutes, representing the deepest cull of any of the tracks retained for the final single album. Clash fans celebrate the song as one of the most audacious world music experiments in a catalog with many similarly commercially challenging examples.

GHETTO DEFENDANT

THE CLASH 4:43

Similar in its weirdly sophisticated reggae vibe to "Car Jamming," "Red Angel Dragnet," "Straight to Hell," and "Atom Tan," "Ghetto Defendant" finds Joe playing beat poet, trading lines with a *real* beat poet, in this case Allen Ginsberg, whom the band summoned to Electric Lady from Boulder, Colorado. Ginsberg stayed for a week and worked on various things with the band, but only "Ghetto Defendant" saw the light of day.

Ginsberg indeed had it in mind to do an album of his own with The Clash as his backing band but instead wound up writing his lines for this imagistic ode to heroin addiction in the broken-down part of the city and in slums all over the world and then purring and performing them as "the voice of God." Arthur Rimbaud is discussed as well (it was said Strummer resembled the French poet), as is the conspiracy theory that heroin is spread intentionally through poor neighborhoods to keep the downtrodden docile—an idea that found new life in America's crack epidemic later in the 1980s.

Nothing much happens musically throughout this slow drip of a track; of main interest are Topper's periodic doubling the speed of the beat along with various bits of ear candy, including a prodigious amount of cowbell, sparse piano, harmonized harmonica, and reverb effects applied to Mick's spare guitar lines. Simply put, if you're not particularly interested in listening to Strummer croon a simple and repetitive vocal melody while Ginsberg interjects with spoken-word fragments, then "Ghetto Defendant" is a frustrating listen indeed.

RIGHT AND BELOW: Combat Rock USA Tour, August 9 to November 27, 1982. The band supported The Who on ten stadium dates.

TOP: The October 13 gig at Shea Stadium in Queens, New York, resulted in a live LP.

INOCULATED CITY

THE CLASH 2:40

On the face of it a perky pop tune, even "Inoculated City" has vague reggae echoes to it. Mick's staccato and repetitive music supports a lyric that is purposely repetitive, each line leading to a restating and summarizing line concerning the futility of war, much in the vein of "The Call Up," both addressing the feeling of powerlessness at the hand of government policy.

The lead vocal has Mick harmonizing with himself over an arrangement featuring two guitar tracks and a bit of keyboards, while Topper keeps time with a disco beat featuring tricky galloping high-hat. A key change at the outro provides a modicum of relief from Mick's sing-songy verse vocal and partial attempt at a chorus—there was more of this in the much longer original mix, as well as an avalanche of spoken-word samples.

If Jones' screed is a bit obvious, especially against the often inscrutable and kaleidoscopic imagery offered by Joe, there's a spot of intrigue in the title, which is perhaps slightly explained with the line, "The jamming city increases its hum," suggesting that by working harder citizens back home are inoculating themselves against the deaths announced on the nightly news. Still, war is discussed in bars and in public bazaars, even if no one understands the conflicts.

Furthering the inoculation theme is a sample of an advertisement for 2000 Flushes toilet cleaner, which suggests the anesthetising nature of television, an idea also explored in "Atom Tan." The band was subsequently threatened with a lawsuit by Flushco Inc. and had to mount a hasty retreat, with CBS pausing manufacture of *Combat Rock* so it could remove the sample from subsequent pressings.

Pretty much limited live to the Lyceum stand in October 1981 and other European dates, "Inoculated City" nonetheless enjoyed some exposure as a B-side to "Should I Stay or Should I Go" for the first of two singles in the United States and the only single in Canada, both non–picture sleeves.

OPPOSITE: New York City, 1983.

DEATH IS A STAR

THE CLASH 3:08

OPPOSITE: The May 28, 1983, US Festival date was Pete Howard's first behind the drum kit and Mick's last with the band. The Clash got in a row with festival security and nearly pulled out to protest inflated ticket prices. They headlined the "New Music Day" over Flock of Seagulls, INXS, and Stray Cats, among others.

Combat Rock's closing selection has the distinction of being the only track that in its final incarnation, was rendered longer than its original on the working-title *Rat Patrol from Fort Bragg* mix. The soft and cinematic song, sort of sophisticated cocktail jazz with a rich and melancholic melody, finds Joe singing quietly, contemplatively, about watching death in film. Joe is mixed hard to the right channel, singing higher up his register than usual; in what stands for a chorus, Mick appears in both channels, double-tracked and singing equally softly and almost romantically about violence.

Tymon Dogg provides an equally light of touch piano, while Topper plays with brushes, at one point laying so far back that only snare vibration is heard, evoking images of a soft rain. Random, occasional finger snaps, fret noise, and delicious pauses add wistfulness to Joe's intimate vocal, the near whisper of a delivery allowing for seamless transition into spoken-word reflections. Crickets and wind chimes open and close the track. The effect is film noir yet peaceable, as if the deaths alluded to are preordained, predictable, part and parcel of the cycle of life.

"Death Is a Star" is an elegant way to end what is sometimes a braying album, with the song's ukulele-like acoustic guitars evoking images of the Spanish Civil War as well as the Roaring '20s, the latter also coming to mind with Mick's piano and Joe's almost Parisian vocal. It is a timelessness The Clash last enjoyed deep within the expanse of *Sandinista!* but most meaningfully within the American songbook traditions of *London Calling*. In that respect, "Death Is a Star," despite its tuck in at the end of the album and subsequent status as an afterthought, just might be The Clash's greatest achievement after 1980.

★ THE CLASH ★

CUT THE C

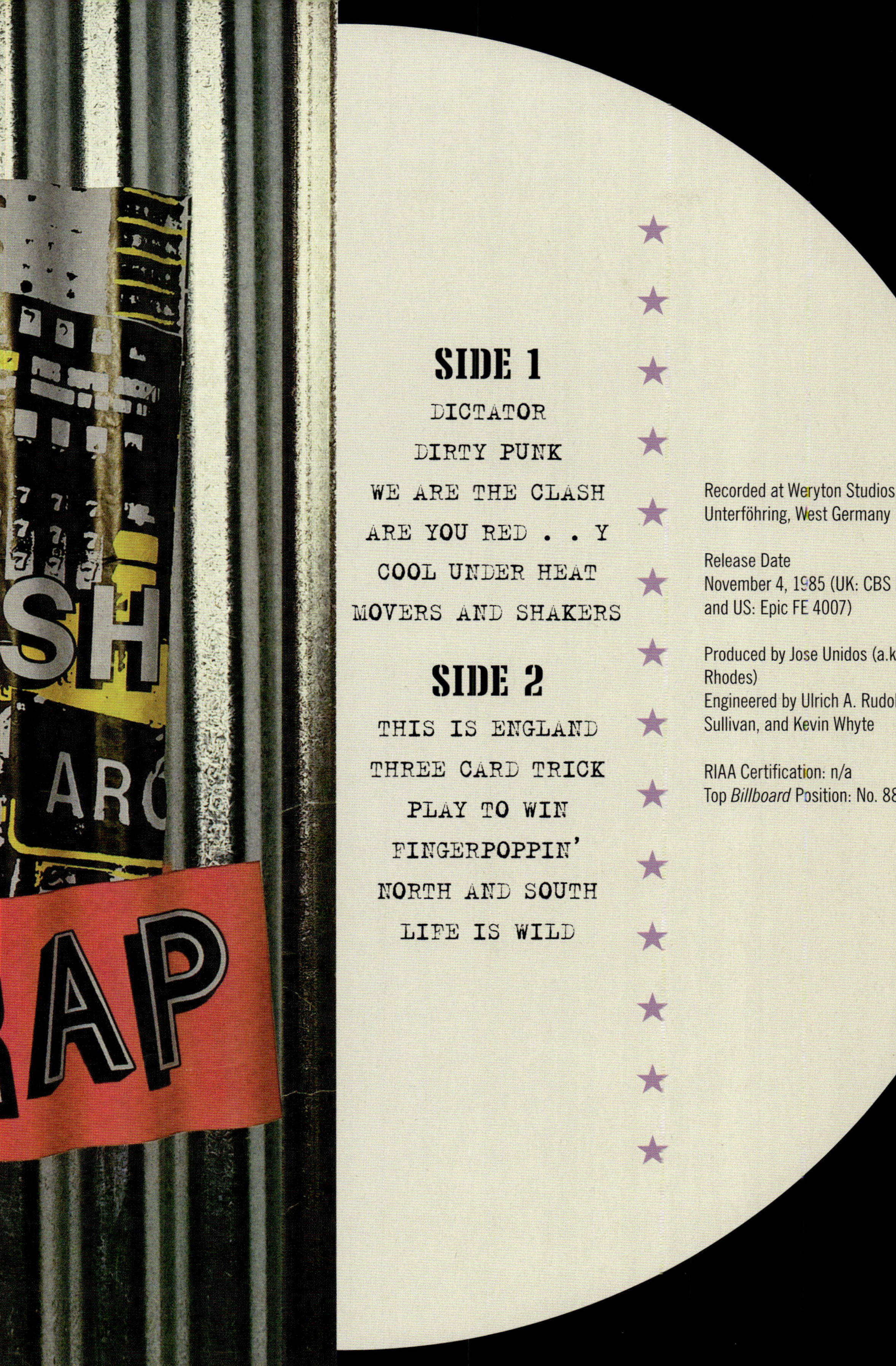

SIDE 1

DICTATOR

DIRTY PUNK

WE ARE THE CLASH

ARE YOU RED . . Y

COOL UNDER HEAT

MOVERS AND SHAKERS

SIDE 2

THIS IS ENGLAND

THREE CARD TRICK

PLAY TO WIN

FINGERPOPPIN'

NORTH AND SOUTH

LIFE IS WILD

Recorded at Weryton Studios, Unterföhring, West Germany

Release Date
November 4, 1985 (UK: CBS 26601 and US: Epic FE 4007)

Produced by Jose Unidos (a.k.a. Bernie Rhodes)
Engineered by Ulrich A. Rudolf, Simon Sullivan, and Kevin Whyte

RIAA Certification: n/a
Top *Billboard* Position: No. 88

CUT THE CRAP

JOE STRUMMER
Vocals

NICK SHEPPARD
Guitar, Vocals

VINCE WHITE
Guitar

PAUL SIMONON
Bass

PETE HOWARD
Drums

GUESTS:
Hermann Weindorf, Keyboards, Synthesizers
Norman Watt-Roy, Bass
Michael Fayne, Drum Machines, Vocals
Bernie Rhodes, Drum Machine Programming

There are those who refuse to accept *Cut the Crap* as a Clash album at all. Notwithstanding such objections, Clash fans are in near unanimous agreement that this lightning rod/kicking post of an album represents a messy and demoralizing end for a great band. With Topper fired for his heroin problem (temporarily replaced by the band's early drummer Terry Chimes), the band eventually picked up the services of Pete Howard, who would last through the *Cut the Crap* cycle. However, Pete was actually in the band for a few months in mid-1983, concurrent with Mick Jones.

By the time the band reconvened to work on a follow-up to *Combat Rock*, Mick had become enamored with synthesizers and was turning in music unacceptable to Joe. It didn't help that Strummer and Jones were also barely communicating as it was, with Mick showing up late for meetings or not at all. Nor did it help that psy-terrorist Bernie Rhodes had returned and was firmly, as always, in Joe's camp (Bernie had changed the title of the last album from *Out of Control* without bothering to tell anyone). The writing was on the wall, and Mick was soon sacked, the band's appearance at the momentous US Festival on May 28, 1983 (New Wave Day) proving to be his last performance with The Clash.

Years later, Mick would muse that his run with the band ended in 1984, the year the band counted up to in the lyrics of "1977," the non-album B-side to first single "White Riot" and a suddenly prophetic song from what seemed like an eternity ago (though it had been scarcely eight years). Some speculation has it that Bernie conspired to get Mick out of the band so he could replace him, most materially as the man in the production chair but also as a writer and band member, possibly goaded on by his rival Malcolm McLaren's spot of success as an artist.

Holding secret auditions, Joe, Paul, and Bernie eventually settled on not one, but two guitarists, with the idea that one was replacing Mick, another Joe, who would henceforth concentrate on vocals. Nick Sheppard and Vince White (actually Greg, but Paul refused to play in a band with someone named Greg!) were brought on board with instructions to get back to punk rock basics and put reggae aside.

Indeed, when it finally emerged, too late for anybody to care, in November 1985, *Cut the Crap* contained no reggae. Buried somewhere behind a wall of chaotic, atonal samples, electronic effects, and drum machines, many of the songs sound like they could have been punk rock anthems . . . had they been approached in just about every opposite way imaginable. And so *Cut the Crap* was anything but back to basics. In fact, with the band's chief music writer gone, replaced by a vague and unwritten combination of Joe and Rhodes, *Cut the Crap* somewhat carries on with the electro-funk trajectory heard on one-third of *Combat Rock* and on songs such as "This Is Radio Clash" and "Cool Confusion." In other words, however unlikely, given the turmoil of its making, the record was actually something of a next logical step from *Combat Rock.*

Upon release, the record was savaged in the press. Even if the band's fan base had been conditioned to expect the unexpected from The Clash, including forward-looking sounds, they'd never been assaulted with electronic drums so obtrusive and noisy (and so obviously *electronic*) on almost every track. Rejection of the album was wholesale, and the band quickly imploded in embarrassment.

Over the ensuing years, fans have salvaged a song or two from *Cut the Crap* they felt could be nursed to health (for this author, it's "Dirty Punk"); for his part, Joe later expressed some fondness for "North and South" and "This Is England." Indeed, "This Is England" has come to be considered something of a Clash classic and is the one song that's been allowed a life beyond the album's dreadful but mercifully short lifecycle.

Unsurprisingly, the rest of the album didn't stand a chance, with anybody who would give it the benefit of the doubt nevertheless condemning it as a demo, given that even this early in the game, smart rock listeners associated drum machines—especially drum machines used by bands with *drummers*—as convenient tools used by writers before the real work began.

But that wasn't the only problem. It was jarring for Clash fans, accustomed to such a steadfast lineup featuring four very distinct, well-known, and beloved personalities, to see the band torn apart, leaving just Joe and Paul. The five-piece configuration was also savaged. The new personnel, the acrimony, the long wait, the noise all over the record . . . it was all too much to bear. *Cut the Crap* would go down as one of the biggest missteps in rock history, made all the more frustrating by the fact there was no supporting tour, no second-act reunion.

And then the was door definitively closed with the unexpected death of Joe Strummer on December 22, 2002, still kicking at the pricks at the age of fifty.

Cut the Crap was savaged in the press. Never had the band's fan base been assaulted with sounds so *electronic* on almost every track. Joe in Southern California, 1984, with new guitarist Nick Sheppard in the background.

DICTATOR

STRUMMER/RHODES 2:59

The Clash Get Out of Control, Philadelphia, April 21, 1984.

It's as if Bernie Rhodes was doing the Malcolm McLaren thing, trying to get a rise, a reaction, assaulting the listener with disparate, ill-fitting noise atop a song too weak to support it. "Dictator" was played live in Europe in the months leading up to the album; on stage, without the drum machine, without the battlefield of samples, it was a solid if midtempo punk track, distinguished by Pete Howard's single-stroke rolls, which, in the context of the lyric, evoked machine-gun fire.

And what of the lyric? Well, it's a surprisingly dull and dead obvious portrait of what a Central American dictator does—an occupation song like *Sesame Street*'s "People in Your Neighborhood." There's no poetry, no pathos, no parallel and ambiguous story line, and none of Joe's scathing and rife specifics—just the rote politics that this is a dictator who will *satisfy the US team*, even that phrase being uncharacteristically stodgy for Strummer.

But the production is the main problem, beginning, of course, with the drum machines, but continuing with the distracting electronic textures, including what sounds like a couple of radios absentmindedly left on in the corner of the studio. A nice idea badly executed is the approximation of a Mexican horn section, while the hardcore hollering on a Clash record is admittedly refreshing, especially when so oddly placed and off-kilter as it is here. The chorus lifts to an intriguing Latin-vibed hard rock, but the verse's arrangement and melody are tired, as is the unremarkable rehash of Clash themes, Joe proving himself to be all out of "Washington Bullets."

DIRTY PUNK

STRUMMER/RHODES 3:07

With a Neanderthal lyric that reads like a parody of a punk song—or worse, a parody of a hardcore song—it's little wonder that Bernie Rhodes mixed Joe's vocal so deep in the mire. But other than Strummer not having anything to say, the song is a barnstormer, the heaviest and most hardcore Clash song ever. Even the drums don't sound so much like a machine as just badly recorded real drums, the life beat sucked out of them by every bad brand-new 1980s toy.

Why the aspiring punk protagonist is so bent on getting the biggest car and driving it "So far up your boulevard" is anyone's guess, but there seem to be some family issues with mother, father, and jock brother behind this decidedly ostentatious and un-punk goal.

New lineup of not-so-dirty punks. From left: Paul, drummer Pete Howard (who actually replaced Chimes before Mick left), guitarists Vince White and Nick Sheppard, and Joe.

But, yeah, the fact is the riffs are killer, from the chugging menace of the verse to the ascending chords of the chorus, the volume of the terrace chants rising with each foisting of a sloshed pint. There's even something of a simple guitar solo, and then it's back to the boot boys hollering about how in an alternate universe The Clash might have gone the way of The Exploited or Discharge or at least the UK Subs, Sham 69, or the Cockney Rejects rather than, as they would say, up their own arses.

Pity that "Dirty Punk" was played live only a couple times, at the Brixton Academy Striking Miner's Benefit Gigs on December 6 and 7, 1984, a lifetime before the launch of the album, on which it would pace alone, impatiently fuming and defiant.

WE ARE THE CLASH

STRUMMER/RHODES 2:58

The somewhat lively drum machine track on this one might not have been so distracting had the guitars not sounded so compressed and processed or if there hadn't been so much sampled noise pollution crammed like cheap mortar between the bricks. In effect, "We Are the Clash" is the dimwit cousin of "Dirty Punk," a little slow and thumpy with a dumpy and goofy riff but still a rousing, pint-swilling good time come the chorus, Joe joining in on the mass of gang vocals, which still manage to be barely discernible above the din. It's really too bad, because the original demo really grooves, featuring more of a Stones-y rock 'n' roll arrangement in stark contrast to the mechanical feel one necessarily gets throughout the album.

"We Are the Clash" was written as an affirmation by Joe, who, after playing a few California dates in January 1984, caught wind that an incensed Mick was telling promoter Bill Graham that he was going to call up Topper and go out on tour as The Real Clash—Topper and Mick were indeed playing together in a short-lived band at this time called Trac. Jones also got his attorneys to freeze remaining payments from the US Festival and some of the residuals from sales of *Combat Rock*. In response, Joe wrote a lyric that was not particularly antagonistic or disparaging but rather almost endearing and innocent, choosing to focus on the fact that he was still out there questioning and taking nothing for granted.

What kind of synth guitar was used for the solo is anyone's guess, but any yabbo with a modicum of punk rock integrity knows the whole idea of a wanky lead break like this is a bad idea (and what's with the bongos?). As if the band realizes that everybody is glancing uncomfortably about the room at this demonstration of bad taste, the song awkwardly and rapidly fades. It's like the power's been cut due to studio abuse.

Joe wrote "We Are the Clash" after catching wind that Mick was planning to call up Topper and go out on tour as The Real Clash.

ARE YOU RED . . Y

STRUMMER/RHODES 2:58

After three stuffy rockers, the new Clash switch channels to a sort of clattery, jittery electro-funk strafed by clean, jazzy guitars as well as uncompromisingly distorted ones. Joe's supporting cast is still there, often hollering *Are you ready for/War?* a less baffling version of the title.

Joe's vocal is delivered in his inimitable rap style, allowing him to rattle off his usual profusion of bon mots (if not his usual quality). The gist seems to be that war is effortlessly international and continental, with limitless reach, due to technological advancements. Mentions of the "red, red phone" and the Kremlin line up with the truncated question "Are you red?," which along with his use of short, fragmented lines, causes further ambiguity as to Joe's message.

As is the case with much of the album, patience wears thin due to the arrangement, the listener fatigued by the braying '80s keys, the turbocharged guitars, military single-stroke snare rolls, and the continued looming presence of soccer hooligans who by now seem camped out on your back patio, singing song after beery fight song. In contrast to the finished product, the demo is pure funk, featuring astringent post-punk chicken-scratch guitars over a fat beat deep in the pocket.

"Are You Red . . Y" was issued as a non–picture sleeve single in Australia, backed with "Three Card Trick," leaving "This Is England" as the only widely distributed single from the album.

COOL UNDER HEAT

STRUMMER/RHODES 3:19

Those brutalizing, compressed, Rockman-like guitars return, especially ill-placed in a song masquerading as a bit of a reggae ballad. Behind the fuzzy electrocution, one can hear strumming acoustics, some wah-wah, bongos, and, once more, a massive angry mob, this time suggesting we try to "Be cool under heat/Be cool on the street."

One can almost imagine those being real drums underneath the sludge, the song being built on a four-on-the-floor bass drum beat without much of a snare presence but real bongos, courtesy of percussionist, programmer, and synth wizard Michael Fayne, who taps out almost too much of a counter rhythm.

In the spring of 1985, manager Bernie Rhodes sent the band on a busking tour of the UK, where Joe and the band found themselves living hand to mouth. Joe and Nick at the Rock Garden in Glasgow, May 15.

Strummer's message struggling to surface amid the din is one of checking yourself before lashing out, in the first verse against economic oppression, in the second while out on the town and up against male aggression, and in the third in disputes of romantic entanglement. Joe's warning at the end seems to be to stay cool or you'll wind up front-page news.

In the spring of 1985, Bernie sent the band on a busking tour of the UK, where Joe and the boys found themselves living hand to mouth and drinking too much, playing in pubs and on the street, but also producing a nice acoustic arrangement of this song that manages to bring out a certain Pogues-like charm missing on the official mix.

IGNORE ALIEN ORDERS

MOVERS AND SHAKERS

STRUMMER/RHODES 2:59

Side one of the original vinyl ends with the album's fourth considerably punked-up rocker of six tracks thus far. "Movers and Shakers" is almost as heavy metal in its verse riff as "Dirty Punk," even if the chorus goes all mariachi with a keyboard line approximating Mexican horns.

Joe's lyric, in direct contrast with his earlier, more incendiary credo proclaiming the right *not* to work, extols the value of hard work. A boy emerges from "the burning slum" and heads uptown to wash cars and make a buck, Joe calling him a mover and shaker, encouraging him to work "coin from the cold concrete" for the time being, even if it's not his bag, and to position himself in good shape for better times ahead.

But the last verse is the most poignant, in which Joe works in his own experience as a squatter and a busker who made good. Anybody with food was a friend and the roof leaked, but they made a drum from a garbage can.

It's not Joe's best lyric, but it's not his worst, either (and it's one of only three selected for printing on the inner sleeve). In fact, it's refreshing that it's not particularly in Joe's typical voice but rather features more literal explanations and descriptions. All told, there's the semblance of a rocking punk 'n' roll song here, Joe goaded into action by yet another stack of gang vocals, although on an aggressive anthem like this, they make perfect sense.

OPPOSITE: Michigan State University, Lansing, Michigan, May 10, 1984.

"THE MEDIA MEAN NOTHING!"

CUTTING THE CRAP WITH BERNARD RHODES

The anarchy surrounding the imploding Clash as they careened toward *Cut the Crap* was the kind of environment in which Situationist-inspired Clash manager Bernard Rhodes was in his element. In fact, just to put an exclamation point on er, Rhodes changed the name of the album without telling anyone—from *Out of Control* to the more confrontational final, underscoring the us-against-them mentality pervading the compromised band at the time. Seeming to anticipate the backlash the album would receive, Rhodes points to a near conspiracy within the press to dismiss the band even before the record could be delivered.

"There was a whole sanction of confusion around that time," reflected Rhodes. "But the media . . . you know, censorship didn't just happen in North Korea, it happened in America and it happened in Europe and the UK, but it was a different kind of censorship. And I always fought against it. The music industry didn't like punk in any way. It embraced it years after, giving it awards. But punk wasn't about getting awards. It was about the audience. And it's quite interesting in politics now how they've suddenly realized there's a voter out there. Whereas before they thought it was just about politicians. So we were always very ahead of the times with our thinking. It wasn't about the Ramones doing versions of the Beach Boys with a bit of Dion, and it wasn't about Talking Heads or Television doing their Andy Warhol thing. It was about the audience, kids out there, taking something from the street and putting it in front of people instead of it going through the media. And that was it. That's the whole of it."

Bernie Rhodes, second from left, with Clash associate Kosmo Vinyl and Mick Jagger backstage at Philadelphia's JFK Stadium on September 25, 1982.

And weirdly, somehow amid all the electronics, *Cut the Crap* was considered by the more charitable critics to be a return to punk or at least a step back from the unraveling reggae sound the band had been collapsing into across the previous two albums. But as Bernie's logic would have it, punk was doomed and had to be replaced, and this was a fight that was apparently still raging in late 1985.

"The whole thing is no more because the media wanted to destroy it and replace it with U2, Green Day, or whatever else, and Broadway shows and Hollywood, you know what I mean?" Rhodes asked. "You got a phony place. The media had had it; they didn't want any punk. They now called it new wave, the Thompson Twins and all that stuff. I'd been in the business since 1958, so the way I look at it is very different to what most people would. And I think it's a disaster the way they took that album. I think *Cut the Crap* is a joyful record. And it's like now, 'This Is England' . . . a filmmaker took the idea and made it into a film, *This Is England*, and then there was a TV series called that. All inspired by this. Massive song, but no one makes that clear."

"My problem is that we had a commitment—to the public, to the record label—to put out a record and go on tour," continued Rhodes, who seems to put some of the debacle down to grit and perseverance despite perhaps the fragile new version of the band not being in a position to make a great record. "That was our commitment. And the fans' commitment was to do what they were going to do. They were going to come or not come. And the record company pay us or not pay us, depending on sales. It was very straightforward. And I thought we had to keep our commitment. And the fact is, that if we had done well, you wouldn't have had U2 or Green Day. *We* would've been the group, do you understand? Paul McGuiness, U2 manager, often said to me, 'Yeah, we always took some ideas here and took some ideas there from you', and that's a reality. But, yes, my job was to keep it going."

Getting around to addressing the biggest complaint folks had with *Cut the Crap*—the use of drum machines for almost all the percussion on the record—Rhodes maintained, "What people misunderstood about it is that it wasn't supposed to be . . . one's always wanted to work with different styles, different attitudes. And that was a continuation. What people got upset about was that it was drum machines. And Joe wanted a drum machine. He said to me, 'I want this record to be drum machines.' That was his brief. Joe said he wanted drum machine, so okay, I'll put an album together around a drum machine.

"And then when his middle-class friends got upset about it, because they were totally into Celtic folk music or whatever middle-class problem they had, he backed off on it. But instead of proudly saying, 'This is good; people won't understand that for a few years, maybe ten years, the next twenty years . . .' But I stick by it. He backed out. Indirectly, but ultimately, I think that led to his disappointment in life and his death. Because he had this nagging him all the time. But Joe, he had a lot of demons to deal with."

As for the new arrivals, namely Vince White, Nick Sheppard, and Pete Howard . . . "They were trying to figure it out," said Bernie. "It's a bit like a sports team. When you get new members in, there's a cultural atmosphere. And new ones come in, new

kids or whatever, and they can't suddenly be stars, can they? But they find their way, and after two or three albums or tours, they might've worked. Who knows? But somehow *Cut the Crap* ended up a really great album. If you put the record on now, you'll enjoy it. It doesn't date. We did it with some very clever ideas that were used later on.

"But I had a concept," said Rhodes in conclusion. "My thing was, best group in the world, best-looking group, group that looked the coolest, that cared about their audience. I want the audience and the group to be one thing. Not a big party but just a bunch of people all together, a rocking community. But you can't have that when the media keep telling the audience what it is and what it's not. And so that's the censorship of it. 'We are The Clash'—it's not about we are The Clash and the other groups are not The Clash. It's about the audience is The Clash. We are like a football team. But it was not understood. There was no enjoyment in finding it out. It was just, 'This is shit, fuck off, let's move on to U2.' Or 'Let's move on to some MOR group.' That's the way to get rid of punk. You destroy it, you undermine it, and unfortunately the people, en masse, went that way. But the media are idiots. The media mean nothing!"

THIS IS ENGLAND

STRUMMER/RHODES 3:47

"This Is England" b/w "Do It Now," UK, September 30, 1985.

Hard to believe, but Joe was so mortified with *Cut the Crap* even before it came out, that once it was done, he said he slunk off to Spain and let Bernie put the record out. Interviews post-release even had Joe denying that it ever came out! The album and this era are not included on the band's official website or in the official film documentary, *Westway to the World*.

"This Is England" was issued as a single all over the world and even reached No. 24 in Britain. Even though the song wasn't considered particularly worthy at the time, over the years it's become something of an admired track, no doubt aided by Joe once calling it "the last great Clash song." Subsequently, it's appeared on *The Essential Clash*, as well as *The Singles*, a CD box set featuring replicas of the band's UK singles.

At the time, however, the song was the only spot of decent news amid Mick Jones and Don Letts getting Big Audio Dynamite off the ground, with debut record *This Is Big Audio Dynamite* issued in October 1985, the month before *Cut the Crap* and slowly rising to impressive UK numbers on the back of three charting singles. Reportedly, Strummer had approached Jones in August to re-form the pre-*Crap* Clash. Ironically, B.A.D. took a tack similar to that being muddled through by the hard-drinking and increasingly erratic Strummer, offering dance beats, synths, and loads of samples. However, B.A.D. had Mick's sense of melody, his voice, a multiracial lineup, and an interesting new sound based on an almost giddy sense of boundless optimism—in other words, B.A.D. were a walking, talking manifesto, while The Clash were no longer really even The Clash.

Musically speaking, "This Is England" is essentially a synth-pop ballad, with soothing synthesizer textures placed over a rudimentary drum machine. Incongruent but by this point, expected, heavy fuzz guitars are introduced. The melody sticks in with the listener not because it's particularly great but because it's melancholic and repetitious. Further, both verses and the chorus are set to the same music, and Joe's unsophisticated vocal melody is easy to sort out.

On the lyrical front, the song wells up with more gravitas than much of the rest of the album, Joe decrying various failures of Margaret Thatcher's England, including the plight of the working class, homelessness, violence, and police brutality. There's also a reference to the bitterly cold winter of 1984, as well as the Falklands War in which Great Britain triumphed over Argentina, resulting in ugly demonstrations of jingoism (the effects of the war still reverberate in the UK—it was a huge political deal at the time, and moreover, resulted in the greatest loss of life for the British military since World War II). There are also a nice few lines addressing the decline, of all things, of Vincent and Triumph motorcycles (iconic British marques), with Joe noting that he has a motorcycle jacket, yet he's walking all the time.

"This Is England" has managed to escape the hoots of derision that rain down on many of the album's other songs because it sounds all right atop electronic drums and is not particularly cluttered with found sounds, the big football chants making sense in the context of the narrative, as do the wistful and bucolic chirps of children at play, their dreams not yet beaten out of them by the England Joe condemns.

"This Is England" was issued as a single all over the world and even reached No. 24 in Britain. Not considered particularly worthy at the time, over the years it's become something of an admired track. Michigan State University, Lansing, Michigan, May 10, 1984.

THREE CARD TRICK

STRUMMER/RHODES 3:06

With "Three Card Trick," Joe cooks up a pleasant enough ska track, and with his vocal melody and performance, as well as the measured use of backup vocals, this one sounds very much like a Clash song. Even the electronic drums aren't too terrible a pox on the proceedings, staying out of the way, as does much of the rest of the uncluttered arrangement, despite a few handclaps and very high-frequency keyboard tones.

This one's lyrics join those of "Dictator" and "Movers and Shakers"; one could only imagine that either Bernie or Joe (or both) were proud of them. Indeed, Joe's treatise is quite serious and bleak, especially against the upbeat ska, Strummer addressing not for the first time on the record the soul-destroying nature of industrial toil (likely with the UK miner's strike at the fore at the time of writing), as well as incarceration, police brutality, and government corruption.

In the end, Joe says that to get by with those in control you *gotta play the three card trick*, likely a reference to the infamous street con game three-card monte recalling the credo of "Cheat" and other songs on the debut that celebrate the outlaw or, more prosaically, carving one's own set of rules to make a mark and a life in a capitalist system seen to be crumbling and stacked against you.

PLAY TO WIN

STRUMMER/RHODES 3:06

Perhaps the most deconstructed and casual sound collage on an album full of bad sculpture, "Play to Win" is essentially noise, bongos, and nonsensical fragmented conversation between Joe and Vince—sampled musings—separated by an Adam and the Ants–evoking chorus pining for "the wild frontier," namely the open prairie, as if both speakers (who were barely speaking to each other) were looking for an escape from the sinking ship that is *Cut the Crap*.

The chorus is belted out in yet another terrace holler, over a non-beat that serves to remind how hobbled the arrangements are all over the album. But that's no surprise, given that Joe, psychologically manipulated by Bernie, was essentially building the record with Vince and Rhodes (Joe admitted that Rhodes indeed did some writing, although not half, as might be suggested by his co-credit on every song) and two German engineers he didn't know but were tasked with most of the drum programming.

What's more, Norman Watt-Roy was playing bass because Paul was away in New York buying paintings and Vince was constantly being mentally torn to shreds by Rhodes, who thought his talents were, well, crap (only Paul seemed to get along with Rhodes by this point, but then again, he didn't have to be around him). Piling on was the fact they were working in a small and unfamiliar demo studio—which, come to think of it, is perhaps why the album sounds like a demo.

Greek Music Festival, Athens, August 27, 1985.

FINGERPOPPIN'

STRUMMER/RHODES 3:22

Backstage at Michigan State University, Lansing, Michigan, May 10, 1984.

Thumping electro drums and fake high-hat do a dance with handclaps and slap bass from Norman Watt-Roy on a song that, again, with different production and playing and arrangement—in other words, a complete rethink, really—could have sounded like a sensible *Combat Rock* track.

Joe's lyric has his finger pointing at the beat, at a brand-new dance, at the prettiest girl in the room—and, he notes, there's no ring on it. The song is essentially an examination of boy/girl dynamics on the dance floor, with Joe chiding both sexes to get up the courage to make that first approach. With all the finger-pointing talk, Joe frames himself as King Confidence, showing these first-timers how it's done.

"Fingerpoppin'" was featured live at the British Miner's Strike benefit at Brixton Academy on January 21, 1985, but that was it. But to be fair, quite a few *Cut the Crap* tracks were gamely trotted out across the band's last doomed dates, all of them being prerelease and of a busking and/or festival nature across the UK, Europe, and an impressive swath of America.

NORTH AND SOUTH

STRUMMER/RHODES 3:28

Arguably a better ballad than "This Is England," "North and South" is for certain one of *Cut the Crap*'s few standouts, given its move through a simple guitar solo section, its clean and fresh keyboards, vocals mostly by Nick Sheppard (with backup support from Joe), and a serious set of lyrics about England's north/south divide, the accusation being that all the heavy lifting is done in the north while the south enjoys the spoils.

Of course, stiff and brash machine bass and snare are all over it, with bongos added as if to percuss all the emotion out of what is a slightly more obscure and thus interesting melodic structure than the one supporting "This Is England."

It's nice to see Joe looking for a ray of hope through Britain's gray dirge, proclaiming the power of protest with the line, "Time can march with its charging feet." He also demonstrates optimism in the idea that the north is no longer digging graves but rather foundations for the future.

Last men standing. Paul and Joe in a Paris press conference photo dated February 1984.

LIFE IS WILD

STRUMMER/RHODES 2:38

OPPOSITE: Fans saw something of a Clash "reunion" in 1986 when Paul and Joe dressed as cops for the video of "Medicine Show" by Mick's Big Audio Dynamite.

Cut the Crap, and thus the wild recorded output of The Clash, closes with a curious thumping party rocker that makes little sense other than to paint the picture of what conversations must be like bar-hopping in the Lower East Side after seventy-two hours without sleep. Indeed, Joe was known for grabbing life by the horns and shaking the stuffing out of it on binges with his many friends the world over, and his lyrics here are both imbued with the energy of drinking and drugging, but they also disturb, with hints of mental illness or maybe just ill choice—as in why such a skilled wordsmith would put these disconnected thoughts on a record.

In that light, it's almost destined and weirdly effective that the song would collapse in a dogpile of noise at the end, the samples winning, drowning out even the most pint-swilling of gang vocal sloganeering. The cumulative effect is of an artificial band barely hanging on by their white knuckles, thrashing out, refusing to go gently into that good night, proclaiming defiantly if also nihilistically that "life is wild, life is free."

ACKNOWLEDGMENTS

A VERY SPECIAL THANK YOU TO PAT GILBERT.

THANKS, ALSO, TO ROB ALFORD, JULIAN BALME, ADRIAN BOOT, JENNY LENS, ANDREW SMYTH, AND FRANK WHITE.

ABOUT THE AUTHOR

At approximately 7,900 (with more than 7,000 appearing in his books), Martin Popoff has unofficially written more record reviews than anybody in the history of music writing across all genres. Additionally, Martin has penned approximately seventy-two books on hard rock, heavy metal, classic rock, and record collecting. He was editor in chief of the now-retired *Brave Words & Bloody Knuckles*, Canada's foremost metal publication for fourteen years, and has also contributed to *Revolver*, *Guitar World*, *Goldmine*, *Record Collector*, bravewords.com, lollipop.com, and hardradio.com, with many record label band bios and liner notes to his credit as well. Additionally, Martin has been a regular contractor to Banger Films, having worked for two years as researcher on the award-wining documentary *Rush: Beyond the Lighted Stage*, on the writing and research team for the eleven-episode *Metal Evolution*, and on the ten-episode *Rock Icons*. Additionally, Martin is the writer of the original metal genre chart used in *Metal: A Headbanger's Journey* and throughout the *Metal Evolution* episodes. Martin currently resides in Toronto and can be reached at martinp@inforamp.net or www.martinpopoff.com.

IMAGE CREDITS

A=all, B=bottom, C=center, L=left, R=right, T=top

Adrian Boot/Urban Image (www.urbanimage.tv): front endpapers; p1; p2; pp4–5; p16L; pp22–23A; pp32–33; p34; p37; p38; p65A; p127; p141; p144; p147; p185; p197T; pp202–203; p233; rear endpapers. **Alamy Stock Photos:** p8T, Nick Moore; p14, Keystone Pictures USA; p83, Trinity/Mirrorpix; p149, Nick Moore; pp154–155, Nick Moore; p158, Michael Brito; p215, Zuma Press Inc.; p219, Pictorial Press Ltd. **Andrew Smyth Collection:** p17L&R; p21BL&BR; p31; p45C&B; p46L&R; p47T&C; p55T&B; p56T&B; p59; p70T&B; p80A; p90BL&BR; p96; p115; p117A; p133; p160; p161T; p177T&BR; p184; p188; p189R; p199; p226T&B. **Author Collection:** p29; p39; p44; p69; p107; p108; p114B; p126B; p131; p161R; p171; p177BL; p201; p221T; p228B. **Bolle Gregmar:** p60. **Chalkie Davis via Getty Images:** p27; p72. **Dean Messina via Frank White Photo Agency:** p209. **Ebet Roberts via Getty Images:** p186; p206; pp222–223. **Frank White Photo Agency:** pp190–191A, Laurens van Houten; p194, Laurens van Houten; p209, Dean Messina. **Getty Images:** p7, Julian Yewdall/Hulton Archive; p9, Dick Barnatt/Redferns; p13, Kypros/Hulton Archive; p19, Julian Yewdall/Hulton Archive; p20, Ian Dickson/Redferns; p24, Kevin Cummins; p27, Chalkie Davis; p28, Julian Yewdall/Hulton Archive; p30, Julian Yewdall/Hulton Archive; p40, Kevin Cummins; p42L, Val Wilmer/Redferns; p43, Kevin Cummins; p51, Michael Putland/Hulton Archive; p53, Michael Putland/Hulton Archive; p54, Julian Yewdall/Hulton Archive; p57, Larry Hulst/Michael Ochs Archives; p58, Larry Hulst/Michael Ochs Archives; p64B, Roger Ressmeyer/Corbis/VCG; p72, Chalkie Davis; p79, Brian Rasic/Hulton Archive; p87, Larry Hulst/Michael Ochs Archives; p90T, Waring Abbott/Michael Ochs Archives; p92, Julian Yewdall/Hulton Archive; p94, Seven Arts/Michael Ochs Archives; p97, Victor Bockris/Corbis; p98, Waring Abbott/Michael Ochs Archives; pp100–101, Peter Still/Redferns; p103, Jorgen Angel/Redferns; p105, Julian Yewdall/Hulton Archive; p112, Peter Still/Redferns; p123, Allan Tannenbaum; p130, PYMCA/Universal Images Group; p134, Janette Beckman; p136B, Ellen Poppinga – K & K/Redferns; p137, Ellen Poppinga – K & K/Redferns; p142, Waring Abbott; p143, Allan Tannenbaum; p148, Henrike Schütz/ullstein bild; p150, Allan Tannenbaum; p157, Bettmann; p166, PYMCA/Universal Images Group; p169T, Waring Abbott; p175, Janette Beckman; p186, Ebet Roberts; p192, Lynn Goldsmith/Corbis/VCG; p196, Dave Hogan/Hulton Archive; p204, Bettmann; p206, Ebet Roberts/Redferns; p213, Ann Summs; p217, Lynn Goldsmith/Corbis/VCG; pp222–223, Ebet Roberts/Redferns; p228T, Chris Walter/WireImage; p229, Eric Bouvet/Gamma-Rapho; p231, STR/AFP. **Jenny Lens:** p68; p81; p84; p99T; p106; p109; p111; pp118–119; p240. **Laurens van Houten via Frank White Photo Agency:** pp190–191A; p194. **Lynn Goldsmith via Getty Images:** p192; p217. **Robert Alford:** p164; p165; p183; p198; p200; p220; p227; p230. **Voyageur Press Collection:** p8B; pp10–11; p15; p16C&R; p18; p21T; p25; p26; p35; p36; p41; p42R; p47B; pp48–49; p63; p64T; p66A; p71A; p73T&B; pp74–75; p77T&B; p83B; p85A; p86; p88; p89; p93; p95; p99B; p110T&B; p114T; p116; pp120–121; p124; p125A; p126C; p128; p136T; p138; p140; p159T&B; p163; p167; p168; p169B; p173; p178; pp180–181; p189L; p193; p195T&B; p205A; p207; p208A; pp210–211; p214; p218A; p221B.

INDEX

ABOUT PM PRESS

PM Press is an independent, radical publisher of books and media to educate, entertain, and inspire. Founded in 2007 by a small group of people with decades of publishing, media, and organizing experience, PM Press amplifies the voices of radical authors, artists, and activists. Our aim is to deliver bold political ideas and vital stories to all walks of life and arm the dreamers to demand the impossible. We have sold millions of copies of our books, most often one at a time, face to face. We're old enough to know what we're doing and young enough to know what's at stake. Join us to create a better world.

PM Press
PO Box 23912
Oakland, CA 94623
www.pmpress.org

PM Press in Europe
europe@pmpress.org
www.pmpress.org.uk

The Clash: All the Albums All the Songs
Martin Popoff

ISBN: 978–1–62963–934–5 (hardcover)
ISBN: 978–1–62963–948–2 (ebook)
Library of Congress Control Number: 2021945056

Art Director: Brad Springer
Cover and Interior Design: Julian Balme at Vegas Design Associates
Layout: Silverglass Design

10 9 8 7 6 5 4 3 2 1

PM Press
PO Box 23912
Oakland, CA 94623
www.pmpress.org

Printed in China

FRIENDS OF PM PRESS

These are indisputably momentous times—the financial system is melting down globally and the Empire is stumbling. Now more than ever there is a vital need for radical ideas.

Friends of PM allows you to directly help impact, amplify, and revitalize the discourse and actions of radical writers, filmmakers, and artists. It provides us with a stable foundation from which we can build upon our early successes and provides a much-needed subsidy for the materials that can't necessarily pay their own way. You can help make that happen—and receive every new title automatically delivered to your door once a month—by joining as a Friend of PM Press. And, we'll throw in a free T-shirt when you sign up.

Here are your options:

- **$30 a month** Get all books and pamphlets plus 50% discount on all webstore purchases
- **$40 a month** Get all PM Press releases (including CDs and DVDs) plus 50% discount on all webstore purchases
- **$100 a month** Superstar—Everything plus PM merchandise, free downloads, and 50% discount on all webstore purchases

For those who can't afford $30 or more a month, we have Sustainer Rates at $15, $10, and $5. Sustainers get a free PM Press T-shirt and a 50% discount on all purchases from our website.

Your Visa or Mastercard will be billed once a month, until you tell us to stop. Or until our efforts succeed in bringing the revolution around. Or the financial meltdown of Capital makes plastic redundant. Whichever comes first.

OTHER PM TITLES OF INTEREST

Stealing All Transmissions: A Secret History of The Clash
Randal Doane
ISBN: 978–1–62963–029–8

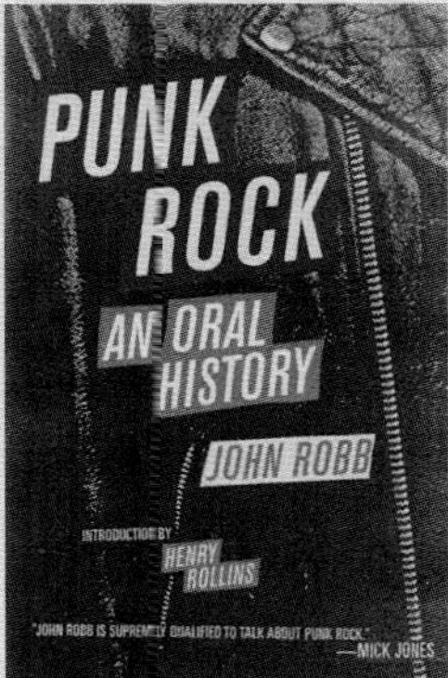

Punk Rock: An Oral History
John Robb
ISBN: 978–1–60486–005–4